From Conflict
to Creativity

From Conflict to Creativity

How Resolving Workplace Disagreements Can Inspire Innovation and Productivity

Sy Landau
Barbara Landau
Daryl Landau

JOSSEY-BASS
A Wiley Company
San Francisco

Published by

 **JOSSEY-BASS**
A Wiley Company
989 Market Street
San Francisco, CA 94103-1741

www.josseybass.com

Jossey-Bass books and products are available through most bookstores. To contact Jossey-Bass directly, call (888) 378-2537, fax to (800) 605-2665, or visit our website at www.josseybass.com.

Substantial discounts on bulk quantities of Jossey-Bass books are available to corporations, professional associations, and other organizations. For details and discount information, contact the special sales department at Jossey-Bass.

We at Jossey-Bass strive to use the most environmentally sensitive paper stocks available to us. Our publications are printed on acid-free recycled stock whenever possible, and our paper always meets or exceeds minimum GPO and EPA requirements.

Library of Congress Cataloging-in-Publication Data

Landau, Sy.
    From conflict to creativity: how resolving workplace disagreements can inspire innovation and productivity / Sy Landau, Barbara Landau, Daryl Landau.
       p. cm.
    Includes bibliographical references and index.
    ISBN 0-7879-5423-3 (alk. paper)
    1. Conflict management. 2. Organizational behavior. I. Landau, Barbara.
    II. Landau, Daryl. III. Title.
HM1126 .L35 2001
303.6'9—dc21   2001003016

FIRST EDITION
HB Printing   10 9 8 7 6 5 4 3 2 1

CONTENTS

This book is dedicated to the many wonderful colleagues, clients, and students who taught us to value the competition of ideas and the cooperation of people.

In particular we want to name one gifted and creative colleague who died far too early and whose life embodied the honoring of diversity, the respectful welcoming of conflict, and the catharsis of humor— especially directed at himself! Daniel Hamoline was the oxygen of so much creativity. We will remember his music and dance in his large footsteps.

PREFACE

This book explores the link between conflict and creativity in organizations. It evolved from work that we have done in conflict resolution over the past twenty years, much of it in organizations. Many of our assignments involve helping work groups to resolve serious conflicts. People in conflict come to us seeking help in getting out of seemingly impossible situations. Rather than provide them with our answers to their problems, we engage them in a collaborative conflict resolution process that helps free them by opening their minds to new possibilities. In other words it helps them be creative.

Time and again what has impressed us is that, when they work together, even adversaries can be more creative than most single individuals could be on their own. Furthermore the solutions developed by the parties are more likely to be supported by the members of the group and therefore are more likely to be implemented successfully.

Our experience is not unique. It is well accepted within the dispute resolution community that collaborative, "interest-based" processes lead to creative solutions. That set us to thinking about the link between conflict and creativity. If a collaborative process involving adversaries who are in conflict can produce results that are more creative than anyone antic-ipated, could a similar process be used to extract creativity from the competing ideas of people who are *not* enmeshed in conflict? Our answer is yes. We use the term *creative con-tention* to describe this process.

AUDIENCE FOR THE BOOK

The primary audience for this book is leaders and members of groups who work together or who meet frequently for the purpose of making common decisions. These groups may take many forms: work units, task forces, project teams, stand-ing committees, boards of directors, hospital treatment teams, and others.

We think this audience will be interested in the concepts we explore for two main reasons: (1) conflict is increasing as work groups are becoming more diverse and organizations are looking for collaborative leaders to manage this diversity in the most effective way; and (2) organizations must become more creative in order to survive and prosper, and conflict is the oxygen of creativity. Without the catalyst of fresh ideas and differing perspectives, change and growth are not possible. Organizations need to offer a climate that fosters and supports creative contention.

Human resource professionals and others who mediate conflicts or facilitate problem solving in organizations will find that this book provides a constructive framework for their efforts. They are often involved in the most challenging situations and need skills to deal with difficult situations after the ability and patience of the leader and the group have been exhausted.

In addition, this book offers students in conflict resolution and organization development an opportunity to understand the links between conflict and creativity and to see how to apply the theory and skills to enhance organizational performance.

CONTENTS AND STRUCTURE

The book is divided into two parts. In Part One we examine unproductive conflict and present a model for resolving disputes not only effectively but creatively. In Part Two we show how organizations can use a similar approach to foster creativity, even when no overt conflict exists.

Part One: How Conflict Can Lead to Creativity

In Chapter One we examine the causes of conflict in organizations, especially the interplay between the diversity of the workforce and the interdependence required among people to get things done. We also explain that organizational conflict is increasing while our tolerance for it is decreasing.

In Chapter Two we discuss the advantages and disadvantages of various strategies for managing unproductive conflict. We present the approach we use to reach win-win solutions in organizations and show how our approach and similar interest-based processes lead to better decisions with more buy-in.

Chapter Three is about the creative resolution of conflict, which is the magical bonus of the interest-based approach. Not only are the results more workable and more acceptable than many other strategies but they are often highly creative as well. We begin to consider the creative possibilities of conflict.

Part Two: Enhancing Creativity Through Conflict

In Chapter Four we discuss the growing need for creativity and innovation in organizations and the reasons group creativity may be preferable to individual creativity. We analyze the links between creativity, diversity, and contention.

Chapter Five deals in depth with creative contention, which is the use of conflict as a catalyst for group creativity. We discuss the four essential components of successful creative contention: (1) a collaborative process, (2) skilled and motivated participants, (3) a leader who is comfortable with conflict, believes in the process, and has the mediation skills to make it work, and (4) a supportive organizational structure.

In Chapter Six we focus on keeping contention creative, that is, on maximizing positive conflict while preventing destructive disputes and dysfunctional relationships.

The final chapter is a summary and allows us to make some observations about the subject matter of the book.

FEATURES OF THE BOOK

We have aimed the book primarily at practitioners rather than academics and thus have focused on practical concepts; wherever possible we have included examples drawn from our experience in organizations, both as participants and as consultants. This seems natural to us because we are not academic researchers; we developed our ideas by applying theoretical concepts to real-life situations.

A few words about our examples: first, each personal example starts with the name of whichever one of us is sharing it. This seems necessary because there are three of us, and we all have different experiences and perspectives. Second, for the most part we have given some information about the organization and industry we are describing, but we have not shared specific identities because of contractual or ethical confidentiality requirements. We believe that our examples are so typical that they will be more powerful if readers use their imagination and insert organizations they are familiar with.

Our roles in the cases we describe vary. In some of the situations we were members or leaders of the groups who were involved in the conflicts or problems. This experience was valuable because it allowed us to experience the situations firsthand. In other cases we were mediators or facilitators. These roles gave us a different perspective: we were able to observe the parties and their interactions from a neutral position.

Finally, we'd like a few words about diversity, conflict, and creativity in the writing of this book. Our central theme is that diversity and conflict are essential for group creativity. Given that the three of us are family members, where is the diversity? To that we answer that we are diverse individuals in many important ways: gender, age (thirty to sixty), personality (introvert-extrovert, structured–laissez-faire), writing style (expansive-spare), professional training (psychology, law, conflict resolution, engineering, business), and experience (corporate, academe, professional practice). We believe that all this diversity contributed greatly to the book. Did we have conflict? Of course. And that, too, helped in this enterprise. By applying the principles of creative contention, we were able to propose and debate our ideas in a collaborative way that provided good, creative solutions that we could all buy into. And we are still talking and creating together.

Sy Landau, Barbara Landau, Daryl Landau
Toronto, Canada
November 2001

ACKNOWLEDGMENTS

We want to thank both of our editors at Jossey-Bass. First, Leslie Berriman kick-started our efforts. Her probing questions and insightful comments helped shape the focus and direction of this book. Her enthusiasm infected us and helped convince Jossey-Bass that conflict is an essential ingredient in creativity and should be seen in both its constructive and its destructive forms. Second, Alan Rinzler added perspiration to our inspiration. Alan has the ability to see both the whole and the parts at the same time, and his observations helped keep us on track and on task whenever our busy lives as conflict resolvers took us on detours.

We want to acknowledge the contribution of our dispute resolution colleagues in Canada, the United States, and around the world, who have inspired us with their dedication to respectful and creative ways of dealing with conflict. Many of them have joined us as faculty in our training programs, and we thank them for the valuable lessons we have learned from them.

We owe a tremendous debt of gratitude to the many clients who trusted us to work with them on challenging organizational and personal issues. We grew from their insights and commitment to building creative and respectful work environments. Many have become friends.

One member of the family did not participate directly in writing this book, but her creative energy, negotiating skill, and incisive questions over the years have sharpened our wits and made us think more carefully about many of the concepts presented here. Niki is an actress and a conflict resolution trainer, as well as Barbara's coauthor on a previous book.

From Conflict
to Creativity

PART ONE

How Conflict Can Lead to Creativity

CHAPTER ONE

CONFLICT IN ORGANIZATIONS

◯

> We all are of two minds about conflict. We say that conflict is
> natural, inevitable, necessary and normal, and that the problem
> is not the existence of conflict but how we handle it. But we
> are also loath to admit that we are in the midst of conflict.
>
> BERNARD MAYER

Conflict exists in all human relationships; it always has and
probably always will. We are continually in conflict with our
parents, our teachers, our partners, our children, our colleagues, and almost everyone else we deal with. This does not
make us bad people or even innately aggressive. Conflict is
natural. It stems from the fact that we each have our own
interests (needs, concerns, goals, and priorities) and are concerned that others may prevent us from satisfying them.

In this chapter we explain that two interacting forces cause
conflict in the workplace. The first is diversity—the fact that

organizations are filled with people with different personal and professional perspectives and interests. The second force is interdependence—the fact that these very diverse people must work together to accomplish their personal and organizational goals. We also consider whether workplace conflict is increasing while our tolerance of it is decreasing.

CONFLICT BETWEEN INDIVIDUALS

Because conflict has been around for so long and is so prevalent today, you might expect that we would accept its presence and be good at resolving it. However, most of us are not comfortable with conflict, and we do not have a broad range of strategies and skills for dealing with it.

We have inherited from our mammoth-hunting ancestors a fight-or-flight approach to conflict. Those of our forebears who survived long enough to procreate did so because they had developed superior skills for fighting or for running away, along with the good judgment to know which approach was called for in different situations.

When we are faced with conflict, most of us (like our forebears) either confront our opponent aggressively in order to win or withdraw from the situation. For most of us these are not strategic decisions; our choice depends, in large part, on our personal comfort level with conflict. Some people are uneasy with conflict and withdraw from it; others thrive on conflict and seek it out.

The fight-or-flight dichotomy that served our ancestors so well is insufficient for our modern needs. It is often socially unacceptable to lash out verbally and usually illegal to strike out physically against our parents, teachers, partners, children, colleagues, or others in society. And running away is seldom the solution. It is unfortunate that many of us have not developed other strategies to replace these outmoded ones.

CONFLICT IN ORGANIZATIONS

It should not be surprising that our discomfort with conflict has carried over into our organizations. Organizations generally hate conflict. Until recently conflict was viewed as abnormal and treated as a shameful corporate secret. In fact, as recently as ten years ago when we offered training programs in organizations, we were often asked not to use the "c-word" in our title. Clients preferred names like "Reaching Agreements That Last" or "Dealing with Differences," as if admitting the need for conflict resolution skills would disclose some serious corporate flaw.

Of course conflict was there. People had opposing interests and different perspectives at work just as they had at home, except that it was unacceptable in most organizations to acknowledge these differences. One reason for suppressing conflict was that managers did not and still do not welcome contrary opinions from their subordinates. Another reason was "company etiquette"; it was more diplomatic to sweep differences under the mat than to risk offending colleagues with whom you had to work every day. Certainly it was bad taste to lose your temper, and emotional responses were usually career inhibiting.

Over the past ten to fifteen years, the situation has improved in that more organizations accept that conflict is natural and not something to be ashamed of. Frontline and managerial employees are more and more often identifying conflict resolution skills as necessary tools for dealing with coworkers, managers, and customers. Perhaps this greater openness reflects the fact that the amount of conflict in organizations is unavoidable and is increasing, for reasons we will discuss shortly.

Conflict is a product of diversity and interdependence (see Figure 1.1). Organizational conflict arises because people who have different personal and professional interests must work together to achieve the organization's goals. Because these people have different interests and may actually be in opposition to each other, they often become concerned that others may block them from meeting their needs.

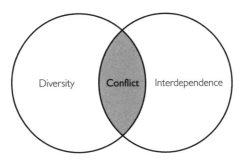

FIGURE 1.1.
Diversity, Interdependence, and Conflict,

DIVERSITY IN ORGANIZATIONS

Organizations are made up of people who have different and quite often opposing values, goals, beliefs, perspectives, interests, personalities, and communication styles. These differences arise from a variety of sources, some personal and some organizational.

Individual Differences
Individuals have unique mixes of personal characteristics and cultural identities that alter the lens through which we view our experiences. Skin color, ethnic origin, socioeconomic class, religious belief, sexual orientation, and physical challenges are some of the influences on our values and outlook. While these characteristics help us connect with other like-minded people, they can also create tension and misunderstanding with those who are different.

7

Other important differences are our personalities and personal preferences. For example, some of us are goal oriented while others are more laid-back. Some of us value high income the most and still others put the highest priority on family life. Some of us like working alone while others prefer working in teams. Some are good with details and others have a broader perspective. And so on.

Professional Differences

In addition to these individual differences there are differences that flow from the professional or functional areas we work in. Marketing people tend to see the world differently from financial people. Human resources specialists often have different values and perspectives than do accountants. This diversity frequently arises because different kinds of people are drawn to different fields of work. It is compounded by the influence that the profession has on the people in it. For example, an outgoing, imaginative, entrepreneurial person is more likely to become a marketer than an accountant. Once in the marketing business, the person will probably be rewarded more for vision, risk taking, and intuition than for caution and accuracy.

Barbara: I was the chief of service of a hospital unit that treated adolescents. The staff came from a wide variety of professional backgrounds, such as nursing, occupational therapy, recreational therapy, psychology, social work, and medicine. Each discipline was totally committed to the well-being of the adolescents, but there was often little consensus on the priorities for care. For example, nurses were concerned about medication schedules, infection rates, and clinical symptoms. Occupational therapists focused on developing job skills and career planning, and arranged outings into the community that played havoc with nursing schedules and, according to the nurses, "exposed clients to infection." Recreation therapists planned strenuous physical activities to occupy the teens in the evening, but unfortunately this was at the point when nursing coverage was at its lowest, creating a risk in case of accidents and also competing with social work's priority of having family visits.

Unclear Vision

When you have many people working in specialized groups, it is important to provide them with a clear idea about the goals, direction, and values of the overall entity. This enables them to carry out their responsibilities in ways that contribute to the success of the enterprise. We need this direction and expect our leaders to provide it. However, when we become leaders we often fail to provide it to others. As a result many people in many organizations are forced to invent their own corporate vision. When you have different versions of goals, direction, and values among different individuals and groups, you increase the probability of unproductive conflict.

> *Sy:* In a museum we worked with, the CEO and the board had not articulated a clear statement of their vision for the enterprise. As a result senior executives were allowed or forced to make their own assumptions. Two key exec-

utives had very different visions, consistent with their own backgrounds and areas of responsibility. One visualized the museum as primarily an educational institution, whereas the other saw its primary goal as entertainment. The business of the museum could not be carried out without the collaboration of these two officers, but unfortunately the difference in their views was a barrier to their cooperation. Their relationship quickly deteriorated and spread to members of their respective staffs. Eventually members of the board became concerned and put pressure on the CEO to resolve the conflict.

Conflicting Responsibilities

Groups are often given responsibilities that are in opposition to those of other groups. To some extent this is inevitable and is in the nature of organizations. Salespeople want to sell as much as they can, and their job is made easier if the product can be customized and the price kept low. Production managers want to keep costs low, and this is best accomplished through long runs of similar items. Finance wants the sales to be profitable, so the price cannot be too low. Everybody is right—to a point. Conflict centers on trying to find the right point. Similar tensions exist throughout all organizations.

Barbara: In one large plant of a public utility, serious tensions developed between the members of one group that operated the equipment and the members of another group responsible for preventative maintenance. The maintenance group had the authority to shut down equipment for maintenance at their discretion. The shutdowns inconvenienced the operators, who doubted the need for many of the shutdowns yet had to work extra time to make up for the closures. The result was serious tension with workplace safety implications.

Unclear Responsibilities

Conflicting responsibilities may be inherent in the nature of organizations, but management sometimes creates additional conflict by being unclear about responsibilities. Even when people have jobs that are quite distinct, overlaps may occur in areas on the margins. An important purpose of job descriptions is to clarify these areas. However, in many organizations job descriptions are several years old, so that even if they were clear when they were written, subsequent developments have rendered them hopelessly out of date. Conflict arises when two or more people, usually acting in good faith, find that they are interfering with one another in carrying out their perceived duties.

> *Daryl:* I was asked to mediate a conflict between a supervisor and his employee. The supervisor wanted to discipline the employee for taking certain actions without waiting for the supervisor's permission. The employee argued that he needed the autonomy to act in crisis situations and that his job description supported his right to do so. Both parties saw themselves as teammates but could not agree on their respective roles and responsibilities.

> *Sy:* In one financial institution a special task force was established to introduce a program of continuous

improvement. There was already an organizational effectiveness group in the company. Nobody clarified where the task force was to leave off and the organizational effectiveness group was to pick up. The resulting bitterness between the leaders of these two groups caused confusion among their clients, and eventually the task force leader had to leave the company.

Conflicting Information

People act on the basis of their understanding of the information available to them. People who have different information or who interpret information differently will act in different ways. Information is not always shared in organizations. Sometimes there are good competitive or legal reasons for this, but it still causes trouble; so does providing complex data without helping people interpret them. Conflict arises because people act on information in ways that others do not understand and therefore misinterpret.

> *Sy:* An engineer employed by a large public utility complained bitterly that his expert advice was not followed in the construction of a large power facility. His recommendations were, he said, "watered down" by people who "knew nothing about" his field of engineering.
>
> When asked who opposed his views, he identified the legal department and the public relations people. He saw their actions as reducing the quality of his work, undermining his authority, and blocking his career development; he even hinted that they might be racially motivated.

When we explored the problem, it turned out that there had never been a sharing of information among the various departments. Everyone recognized that the engineer had the necessary expertise to make decisions about technical matters. However, he did not realize the difficulties his decisions would have created by breaching zoning and environmental regulations or the uproar in the media from environmental activists and local citizens who were concerned about the impact on local habitat and on real estate prices. His frustration could have been alleviated and a plan devised that better met the broader range of interests if all relevant parties had shared information and discussed all of the consequences.

All of the types of diversity described in the preceding examples created the *potential* for conflict. The left circle in Figure 1.1 (p. 7) represents this diversity. If the people holding diverse views had been working independently, conflict would not have arisen. Conflict emerged because these very different people had to work together (see the right-hand circle in Figure 1.1).

INTERDEPENDENCE IN ORGANIZATIONS

In simpler times it might have been possible for people to work independently on their own tasks. A craftsman could work alone to create his product; a saleswoman could call on customers by herself to sell merchandise; an accountant could single-handedly prepare statements; a health professional in a hospital could, without assistance, treat a patient with a particular need.

This kind of independent activity may still be occurring in some small enterprises, but it is the exception, not the rule. In order to meet the complex challenges facing them today, most organizations must bring together skilled and motivated people from a variety of backgrounds and encourage them to work collaboratively to meet common organizational goals. Marketers, salespeople, designers, craftsmen, and financial experts must work together to create products that can be sold profitably. Salespeople often have to bring designers or financial experts on sales calls in order to sell complex products. Health care professionals now work in multidisciplinary teams to ensure that patients receive more holistic treatment. This combination of diversity and interdependence gives rise to conflict.

If we study the examples of diversity, it becomes obvious that although the differences were necessary contributors to the conflict, they were not sufficient. In each case if the people holding the different views had worked in separate settings, their differences might have provided the subject matter for interesting mealtime or conference debates, but they would not have been in conflict with one another. It was the need to take unified actions that made the conflict real. Barbara's team of diverse professionals had to agree on plans for managing the same group of adolescents. The engineer could not implement his ideas without the concurrence of the legal and public affairs people who saw things very differently. The continuous improvement task force and the organizational effectiveness group worked for the same company on similar issues.

Many factors compound the effect of interdependence. One is the competition for scarce resources. Another is the struggle for power. Yet another may be the organizational structure itself.

Scarce Resources

In most organizations the demand for people, equipment, and money exceeds supply. This could be because resources are actually short or because there is an abundance of ideas on how to use them. Regardless of the reason for it, the result is a belief among members that their personal and professional objectives will be thwarted because other people will be given "their" resources. This often results in colleagues undermining or even sabotaging each other to ensure that they get the resources they need.

> *Sy:* A group of news producers working for a small television station were in a continual state of conflict with one another. Their whole work day was filled with the competition for scarce resources: who would be assigned the

high-profile story, who would get the most competent camera person, who would get first crack at the limited editing facilities, and whose story would get the best and the most air time.

Power Struggles

Despite efforts to flatten out structures, most organizations are still hierarchical. Position in the hierarchy conveys the power to affect how things get done, so people with agendas and ambition covet key positions. These people quite naturally view their colleagues as potential roadblocks to their careers. Thus people behave competitively when they should be cooperating in the corporate interest. Management often encourages such competitive tendencies out of a belief in natural selection.

> *Sy:* Several years ago some tenured faculty members at one of the campuses of a large state university system anticipated funding cuts that could lead to reductions in the faculty. In order to reduce their own vulnerability, they decided to block tenure appointments in areas that might be valued more than theirs. A few of these plotters managed to be appointed to the tenure committee and began to implement their plan. The resulting conflict eventually required the intervention of the academic vice president.

Organization Structure and Procedures

The organization structure itself can cause conflict. Structures formalize and rigidify the way people are supposed to work together. A structure that forces people to work together who have opposing or ambiguous responsibilities creates "rub points" that cause raw wounds.

Sometimes organization structures that once made sense have not kept pace with changes in direction or strategy; sometimes the structures never made sense at all. Perhaps a structure was designed to take advantage of the strengths of a particular individual, or to compensate for someone's weaknesses, or to keep two incompatible people apart. Those people may no longer even be in the organization. Whatever the reasons, there is a saying: "If you put good people in a bad organization structure, the bad structure will win."

Barbara: In one organization a conflict between two departments had continued unabated for about nineteen years. At the time of our involvement, almost none of the original staff remained, but the conflict persisted. One department was responsible for the design and construction of equipment, and the other was responsible for operating and maintaining the equipment. The two departments should have been working closely together; in fact, they had no formal contact.

The two managers who had led the departments nineteen years before had been unable to get along, and senior management had decided that the solution was to have each department report to a different vice president. The structure of the organization was changed, and the conflict apparently disappeared.

However, by the time we were called in, the two departments were in public competition with each other. Over the years both had hired additional staff to replicate the work of the other rather than work with their "rival." Customers were playing one department off against the other, and complaints to the head office were increasing. The organizational structure that was intended to solve the problem was now causing dysfunction because it hampered communication, left customers unhappy, and added unnecessary expense to the organization.

Sometimes it is not the structure that causes problems but the systems, rules, and procedures that are either out of date or nonexistent.

Daryl: A young educational institution had not created the systems for handling discipline problems with students. Neither did they have hiring procedures for staff or decision-making procedures for the many unresolved problems in the school. The lack of structure opened the door to power struggles between the administration and the teachers. The power struggles fueled racial divisions among the staff. As a result the future of the school was jeopardized.

PERCEPTION VERSUS REALITY

We have shown that conflict in organizations arises because people with different interests must work together, yet worry that others will block their interests. Sometimes our perceptions are accurate, and sometimes they are not. When it comes to conflict, reality is not nearly as important as perception. Two people who believe that they have opposing interests will behave as if they do, even if their perception is wrong. People who expect others to block their goals will react according to their expectation, whether or not it is based on fact.

Sy: One of the most contentious cases we have worked on involved serious, life-threatening conflict between several members of a heavy-equipment maintenance department and the foreman. The triggering incident occurred during a bitter strike. The employees perceived that the foreman had played favorites in selecting the "essential workers" who would continue to work while the others earned strike pay and walked the picket line in freezing winter weather. The disgruntled workers began to show disrespect to the foreman. They filed grievances for every minor concern. Their motto became, "If he moves, grieve." The foreman reacted to the employees' initial actions with equally hostile behavior, other employees took sides, several death threats were sent, and the grievance process became bogged down in charges and countercharges.

Our investigation two years later found that the foreman had played no role in the selection of essential workers. That had been done at the head office using a formula. The whole mess had started with an unverified misperception. Of course by this time much water had flowed under the bridge, the conflict had escalated beyond the .

initial issue, and many other people had been drawn into the conflict.

This example illustrates the typical conflict "cycle," shown in Figure 1.2. Assume that two people (Alice and Bob) are in a reasonably good working relationship until the following series of steps take place.

1. Alice forms a belief that Bob has opposing interests and is therefore likely do something to block her interests.

2. Alice takes some action designed to promote her interests at Bob's expense.

3. As a result of Alice's action, Bob perceives, perhaps for the first time, that there is a conflict between them.

4. Bob takes some retaliatory action designed to promote his interests at Alice's expense. Alice views Bob's action as corroboration of her initial perception, and this justifies another round of actions.

Thus the cycle is really an upward spiral of actions, perceptions, and counteractions.

Misperception often results from a failure to communicate. When we do not clarify our intentions, explain our actions, check our assumptions, or listen carefully when others try to explain, we risk setting in motion a conflict cycle that escalates out of control.

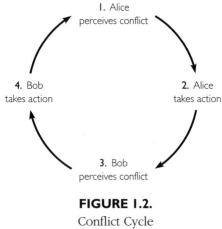

FIGURE 1.2.
Conflict Cycle

IS ORGANIZATIONAL CONFLICT INCREASING?

The conditions described in the preceding section have existed for many years, as has the resulting workplace conflict. There is a lot of anecdotal evidence that potentially destructive conflict is growing in the workplace:

- Organizations that ten years ago would not admit to the presence of conflict now schedule regular training programs in conflict management for managers and staff.

- Grievances, lawsuits, and wildcat strikes seem to be increasing.

- The news carries all-too-frequent reports of violence by employees who have become enraged by unresolved conflict with their peers or managers over real or perceived insults, fears for their future, or lack of recognition.

- At several conferences and training programs we have asked people if they are experiencing more workplace conflict, and the affirmative response is almost unanimous.

In reaction to this growing conflict, managers are identifying conflict resolution skills as critical competencies for themselves and their subordinates.

Many factors contribute to the growth of conflict within organizations. We discuss some of the common ones in the sections that follow.

Increasing Workforce Diversity

Earlier in this chapter we demonstrated that diversity in the workplace creates the potential for conflict. It seems obvious that the workplace is becoming more diverse in many ways. Here are a few of them:

1. Women now make up about 40 percent of the North American workforce, with increasing representation in management and other nontraditional roles. For various reasons women

often see and do things differently than men. Society also places different expectations on men and women.

2. Age diversity is increasing. Although early retirement options have increased, many people are working longer because they have to or want to. In some fields people work into their seventies. People at or near retirement or working in semiretirement may have very different expectations and interests from their younger colleagues. Corporate loyalty, long-term employment, job security, and pension benefits are likely more important to older workers than to the generations that follow. However, many younger people seem to want less structure and more informal dress; many prefer to work from home.

3. Organizations are including more people of different professional or specialist backgrounds. In most enterprises one can find salespeople, product designers, public affairs experts, human resources professionals, engineers, computer specialists, financial analysts, lawyers, and so on. These people tend to see the world differently and sometimes have difficulty accepting the perspectives of others.

4. North American society has long been a society of immigrants, and today's immigrants come from more diverse parts of the world and bring with them a wider variety of traditions, expectations, and behaviors than in previous generations.

5. Globalization increases the interactions among people from different parts of the world who work in different business cultures and experience different national loyalties.

People of different cultures, genders, ages, and professions may have different attitudes toward work and family, equality and independence, individuality and teamwork, merit and seniority, and countless other factors that can cause tension among colleagues or between managers and subordinates. There is no question but that these differences complicate working life. Even holidays can become issues. For example, when the workforce was relatively homogeneous, organizations could simply decide to close down at Christmas and Easter. Now an increasing proportion of the workforce expects time off for other non-Christian holidays.

Increased Interdependence in the Workforce

The increasing use of teams, especially multidisciplinary teams, means that we are spending more time working on tasks with people coming from different professional backgrounds, representing different constituencies, or having different perspectives. Individuals on a team may have different objectives, priorities, or values.

Barbara: One hospital we worked with relies heavily on multidisciplinary treatment teams, bringing together physicians, nurses, social workers, speech pathologists, dieticians, and others to treat elderly patients with certain types of disorders. Hospital management and team members recognize the value of the multidisciplinary approach, and most try to make teams operate effectively.

Despite good intentions difficult problems arise. For one thing, team members bring with them baggage from their allegiance to their professional disciplines. And as representatives "on loan" from professional departments, they frequently have to justify team decisions to their professional colleagues. Another issue is that most team members belong to powerful professional colleges that enforce rigorous standards of practice. Because these standards of practice differ from one another, team members are frequently faced with conflicts over which standards apply. Furthermore there is a (formal and informal) hierarchy in the hospital, and this often breeds resentment. Team members from less prestigious specialties are sometimes reluctant to speak out, even when they are more familiar with the patient or the work of the team.

Add to these factors the individual differences in personality, language, communication skills, and so on, and the potential for conflict is obvious. And of course very few members of the teams have had conflict resolution training. As a result some teams are rife with conflict. Some of it is displayed openly in team meetings. More of it is discussed within cliques outside the meeting rooms or back in professional departments. Some members ask to be reassigned because of the stress of the unresolved conflict.

More Mergers and Strategic Partnerships

Mergers, acquisitions, and partnerships have similar effects: we have to work together to achieve goals that may be common in theory but are really in opposition, at least in some important ways.

> *Sy:* I was involved in the merger of two financial institutions or, more accurately, the acquisition of a smaller company in another city by our larger one. We established joint teams to plan and coordinate the merger of departments. Teams were expected to evaluate the systems and processes of the duplicate departments and assess the relative qualifications and productivity of their staff. We were to determine which possible location best served the needs of the merged company and its customers.
>
> In theory team members were working toward common organizational objectives, but in reality our personal interests were often in opposition. We all understood that decisions about systems, processes, staff, and location would ultimately affect our own roles, status, families, and personal lives—even our continued employment.
>
> I remember overhearing a discussion between our CEO and one of our vice presidents. The CEO said, "After all, we want the best people to head up all divisions, regardless of which company they come from, don't we?" The VP responded, "Of course!" But I could tell that he was really thinking, "Of course, as long as it's me."

Competition for Resources

Global competitive pressures require organizations to accomplish more challenging goals more quickly, often with fewer people, tighter budgets, and more limited resources. Organizations are not just competing with other local or national enterprises that are subject to similar constraints and regulations but they are competing with companies that do not have to play by the same rules.

Parts of organizations find themselves in competition with other parts of the same companies. The auto industry is a good example. Plants must bid against one another for the rights to build new models. The losers are closed down. This may be good for the business and may even be necessary for survival, but it definitely creates conflict.

IS TOLERANCE OF CONFLICT DECREASING?

At the same time that organizational conflict is increasing, our tolerance of it and our patience for resolving it may be declining. Even when we are at our best, most of us view conflict as a nuisance—an unwanted condition that interferes with our ability to carry out our responsibilities. However, if we add the pressures of time demands, constant change, and insecurity about our jobs, most of us are not at our best.

Time Pressures

Most of us are experiencing time pressures caused by some combination of meeting increasing demands at work and at home with less help. Although many organizations espouse the value of balancing work and family, employees at all levels perceive that trying to achieve this balance will hurt their career prospects.

> *Sy:* The senior executive of the financial area of a large company asked us to explore the reasons for the morale problems in his area. One of the things we discovered was that people resented the long hours routinely expected of them. Our client was surprised because both he and the CEO had frequently emphasized their commitment to work-family balance. It was written into the company's policies. However, employees told us that it was difficult to leave work at a reasonable time when their managers worked regularly into the evening. They also said that staff reductions meant that they could not leave at normal times and still get their work done within the established timeframes. These people "did not have time" for anybody who made other demands on them or raised contentious issues.

Constant Change and Job Insecurity

Constant change is another factor that is putting us on edge. In the past, life could be viewed as a relatively tranquil river, interrupted periodically by areas of "white water" that had to be navigated carefully in order to safely reach the next long stretch of calm.

Today change has become the constant white water of our lives, especially our working lives. If we are lucky enough to still be afloat at the end of the rapids, we know that the next set of rapids is just ahead.

None of us can really feel secure in our jobs anymore. Global competition keeps raising the performance bar, requiring us to run faster just to stand still. Even companies with healthy bottom lines are not immune from the pressure for continuous improvement. Because we lack confidence in our future prospects, we view our colleagues as potential competitors, reducing our willingness to collaborate with them.

Even if we perform well enough to beat back the individuals competing for our job, our job might disappear because our employer introduces new technology that makes us obsolete or closes down our division or location because of a new strategy. Or our employer might disappear because of a takeover by another corporation. We do not need to be paranoid to perceive that a lot of other people are pursuing their own interests without regard to us and that they might do us harm.

> *Sy:* I have an account with a bank in South Florida. It seems
> like every few months I get a letter from another bank
> telling me that it has just bought out my previous bank. I
> am still using the checkbook from three banks ago. I

know nothing about the inner workings of the institutions, so I don't know how all of these changes have affected their employees, but I doubt that any of these takeovers were intended to protect the status quo within the organizations.

EFFECTS OF ORGANIZATIONAL CONFLICT

As we have discussed in this chapter, conflict in organizations is natural and inevitable. It is also increasing. If conflict is not resolved, the result can be a poisoned environment in which people are afraid to raise important issues because they might be contentious and every issue that does surface becomes a divisive dispute.

However, we should not be overly concerned about organizational conflict because the real issue is not its presence but how it is handled. If conflict is managed effectively, the workplace can be a pleasant and stimulating environment. In fact, it can even be very creative, as we discuss in depth in Chapter Three and in Part Two.

In our experience an effective organization is one in which conflict is expected, surfaced, and managed promptly and well. In the next chapter we discuss how conflict can be resolved.

CHAPTER TWO

MANAGING ORGANIZATIONAL CONFLICT

◯

Figuratively, if not literally, the participants should come to see themselves as working side by side, attacking the problem, not each other.

ROGER FISHER AND WILLIAM URY

In this chapter we discuss the advantages and disadvantages of various strategies for managing unproductive conflict in organizations, both in terms of the results and the relationship between or among the parties. We show why a collaborative strategy is the best approach in most workplace situations. We present the approach we use to reach win-win solutions in organizations and show how our approach results in better decisions with more buy-in and may even transform the relationships between the parties.

CONCERNS IN RESOLVING CONFLICT

You can pay attention to two things when you are in conflict: results and relationships. If you focus on the topics you are in conflict *about,* you are concerned about *results.* If you focus on the people you are in conflict *with,* you are concerned about *relationships.* When you are striving for results, you concentrate on putting forward your needs and preferred solutions. When you are focusing on relationships, you concentrate on listening to others' views and cooperating with them.

Disputants often see this as an either-or choice: either they are arguing for their own needs or they are cooperating to meet the other person's needs. Many believe that if they show a concern for the relationship, it will appear as a weakness and undermine the pursuit of their objectives. Others think that if they insist on meeting their objectives, they will damage the relationship. It requires a new mind-set to realize that the two areas of concern are independent of one another, that is, *you can put a lot of effort into meeting your important needs and at the same time preserve significant relationships by attending to the important needs of others.* This is the paradigm shift that creates win-win, high-quality outcomes.

There are five different approaches to dealing with conflict, depending on the amount of attention paid to results and relationships. The approaches are illustrated in Figure 2.1, which is based on the Thomas-Kilmann Conflict Mode Instrument (1974).

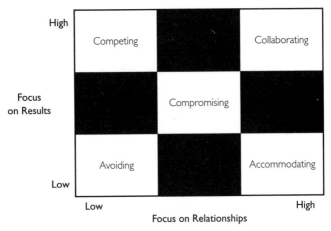

FIGURE 2.1.

Approaches to dealing with conflict

Avoiding

When we ignore or withdraw from conflict, we are neither trying to achieve substantive results nor addressing relationships with other people. We simply do not want to deal with the conflict. Although this approach may buy us some short-term peace and in a few cases may allow problems to go away on their own, it has some serious drawbacks: unresolved conflicts often get worse; decisions may be made by others, and we may not like the decisions; people who depend on us might get frustrated by our lack of action; and our reputation (and career) might suffer.

> *Sy:* In Chapter One I described a conflict between two senior executives in a museum. The reason the situation had reached the point at which members of the board

had become aware of it and had insisted that something be done was that the CEO was a conflict avoider. His inaction in the early stages of the disagreement over direction had permitted the conflict to escalate and get out of control.

Competing

People who concentrate exclusively on results are said to be *competing*. They often do so out of a belief that, in resolving conflict, someone must win and someone must lose—and winning is better. In many organizations managers are expected to take a competing approach with their employees. For example, managers might wield their authority to make decisions without considering the input or interests of their subordinates (power-based conflict resolution). Or they might use the policy and procedures manuals to get their way (rights-based conflict resolution). This may be seen as decisiveness. Unions also play hardball by filing grievances (rights-based) or threatening job actions (power-based). Neither rights-based nor power-based approaches achieve satisfactory results, with buy-in from all parties.

Organizations often use competing tactics when dealing with suppliers or even customers by enforcing contracts in the courts or threatening to sever working relationships. These tactics are used even in situations where this is neither the best option for the buyer nor the most reasonable approach for the supplier.

People who take a competing approach rarely consider the implications. They do not think about the damage they may be doing to the long-term relationship with the other parties. This may make it harder to meet their needs in the future. It is ironic that they may be impairing the immediate results that they believe are so important. By failing to take the perspectives of other people into account, they may come up with incomplete results. And by not considering the interests of the others, they will not be likely to get their cooperation in making the solution work.

There are times when competing is an appropriate strategy— when achieving the "right" result is so important that it overrides everything else. An example of this for most of us would be when people's safety is at stake. However, most instances of competitive conflict resolution have nothing to do with survival.

> *Daryl:* A supervisor in a public institution was taking a very tough line in a dispute with his employee. He expected his employee to follow orders, "end of discussion." He insisted on his right to discipline his employee for not doing things by the book. This approach lost the supervisor the respect of his own boss, who felt there was no legitimate basis for disciplinary action. Human Resources voiced the same concerns. The supervisor was isolated. Management had to choose which of the two (supervisor or employee) should remain in his current position and

chose to transfer the supervisor. In the end the supervisor's competing stand lost him his position.

Accommodating

Accommodating means putting other people's needs ahead of our own, that is, being prepared to forego meeting our substantive interests in order to build a good relationship with other people. Sometimes this is wise. For example, it may be wise when the substantive results are really not that important compared with the long-term benefit of a strong relationship (such as with important customers) or when we might as well give in to a more powerful opponent and thus gain some credit for future use.

We have found that organizations include a disproportionate number of accommodators. This feeling that you have to "go along to get along" puts a high value on harmony. The trouble is that accommodators often give up important substantive objectives, which they later regret. And they often do not get the appreciation and relationship they crave. They also risk losing the respect of their colleagues if they accommodate too much and may become known as easy marks.

In problem-solving situations accommodators may not put forward their own ideas out of a concern that others may be offended. Therefore the organization may suffer because the accommodators' input might have contributed to better decisions.

Compromising

Compromising means trading off some things of value to gain other things of value. When people compromise, each person partially meets the other's demands. This is frequently more satisfying than trying to force your optimum solution on others and thereby damaging the relationship or sacrificing all substantive objectives in order to make others feel good. Compromise leaves everyone with something, and it need not take much time.

However, compromise has a better name than it deserves. Many people think that compromise is the ultimate goal in dispute resolution. They may not realize that compromising can often mean sacrificing important needs. It is not unusual for both parties to walk away unsatisfied from a compromise, wondering if they really had to give up those interests.

If parties in conflict know that the resolution will be reached through compromise, they may be tempted to make higher initial demands so as to end up with more of what they really want after the trade-off. If both parties do this, the process ends up driving them further apart each time. It gives a cynical appearance to conflict resolution.

> *Sy:* I was recently involved in renegotiating a labor contract.
> Relations between management and the union have
> been cordial for years. The union kicked off the bargain-
> ing process by handing management a list of demands.

Among other things, the union was asking for more than an 18 percent salary increase over the three-year contract. The surprised management negotiator asked the union rep for some rationale behind the seemingly high demand. The union rep chuckled and said, "Creative math. You can't blame someone for trying." The contract was signed with a salary increase of less than half that initially demanded. The unreasonable position taken and the attempt at manipulation undermined management's trust in the union rep and created skepticism about subsequent offers. It did harm the relationship and could have an effect on future negotiations. There might even be some immediate fall-out for the union. If its members actually believed that the 18 percent salary demand was realistic, they will be disappointed in their leaders and possibly rebellious.

Collaborating

If both results and relationships are important, collaboration is the most useful approach. In order to reach a collaborative solution, all parties must carefully and respectfully explain their own needs and concerns and listen actively to the needs and concerns of others. They then try to construct a solution that meets everyone's needs. The solutions tend to be reasonable because everybody's input has been considered. Relationships are enhanced when all parties feel that their interests have been listened to and met to the fullest practical extent. And the solutions are likely to be implemented because it is in everyone's interest to do so.

Collaborating may take longer than compromising to reach an agreement because collaborating involves deeper discussions and more problem solving. It may take longer than imposing your way on others through power or rights (unless you are up against another strong, competitive person), and it certainly takes longer than giving in or withdrawing. However, collaborative solutions are usually implemented more quickly and last longer, and this more than makes up for any extra time taken in problem solving.

Another important way in which collaboration may achieve more efficient results is that participants expend their energies on problem solving rather than blaming. Competers tend to bog down in mutual attributions of fault, whereas collaborators rarely waste time or risk damaging the relationship by pointing fingers. Our observations repeatedly reinforce the fact that collaborators look at what is possible; they are future oriented and focused on solving the problem while preserving goodwill.

We have used an assessment instrument with several thousand people in organizations over the past fifteen years, and we find that collaboration is underused. This is not because of strategic selection as much as a lack of awareness and a lack of skills. Our experience is that collaboration should be the first approach considered. Only if other approaches have a more compelling strategic purpose should they be used.

Collaboration is the foundation of most of the processes we present in the rest of this book.

Collaboration neither replaces managerial accountability nor turns every decision into a group decision. Collaboration simply means that decision makers consult with and problem solve with other knowledgeable and affected stakeholders and strive for consensus. If the group cannot reach consensus, the leader decides. That decision will usually be better and more acceptable than an autocratic ruling. In an article in *The Globe and Mail* writer Natalie Southworth (2000) reports that some management experts believe that "being able to work collaboratively—delegating responsibility and appreciating diversity—is becoming the way of the New Economy" (p. B8). (The article goes on to say that U.S. firms are seeking out Canadian CEOs because they tend to be more collaborative than the "traditional U.S. style of leading the troops over the hill to conquer" [p. B8]). With the increase in stress and turnover, especially among young people, managers would be wise to consider more collaborative approaches that build loyalty based on a feeling of making a personal contribution to the organization.

Barbara: I was the chief of service of a hospital-based treatment unit. The hospital faced severe financial constraints, and every unit was asked for cost-cutting measures. A number of my colleagues put forward proposals that they had developed on their own or with a small management team. Instead I set aside two days for the entire staff to work together on a strategic direction and a strategic plan for our unit that would meet the fiscal objectives and still meet our clients' important needs. The result was a wonderfully creative shift in treatment delivery that had the full support of staff and could be implemented with minimal delay; it also saved the hospital money. The results exceeded expectations and left me secretly grateful for the incentive to conduct this collaborative process.

COLLABORATIVE CONFLICT RESOLUTION

In organizations both results and relationships are important; organizations exist to produce results through the combined efforts of their members. Problems should be solved in ways that promote the competition of ideas while encouraging the cooperation of people. This is the essence of collaboration.

Our approach for resolving organizational conflict consists of three stages:

Stage 1: Determine the underlying causes of the conflict. In particular determine whether or not interpersonal issues are significant contributors to the conflict.

Stage 2: Deal with significant interpersonal issues first.

Stage 3: Then resolve the substantive issues.

We will explain the stages one at a time in the sections that follow.

Stage 1: Determine Causes

Many workplace issues are primarily interpersonal. The main problem is that the particular players are not prepared to work together to solve problems. In fact, they often turn small substantive issues into big problems because of their interpersonal conflict. Very often interpersonal issues are disguised as substantive issues.

> *Sy:* In Chapter One I described serious, life-threatening conflicts in a heavy-equipment maintenance area. When we were called in, there were disputes between employees and the foreman and between employee cliques over issues like overtime allocations, job assignments, and promotions. Although these are substantive issues, the real problem was that the parties did not trust or respect one another. Therefore they were unwilling to deal in good faith with issues that otherwise could have been resolved easily. The substantive issues could only be addressed after the interpersonal animosity had subsided.

Other issues are primarily substantive, that is, they are about finding solutions to work problems when there are several different opinions about how to proceed. Examples might include what price to charge for a new product, whether or not to open a branch in a new location, what the best treatment for an ailing patient is, and so on. These problems would have to be solved regardless of who the decision makers are.

Barbara: A large hydroelectric company was undergoing a major reorganization. There was public pressure to come up with a more efficient, cost-effective, and environmentally friendly way of delivering electric power to a large geographic region. In the past a variety of divisions acted relatively autonomously, and the desire was to develop an integrated plan with a well-thought-out business rationale. This was largely a substantive problem, although the changes proposed would have broad effects within and outside the organization.

Many conflicts consist of a combination of substantive and interpersonal issues. There are important and complex business or professional issues to address, but the interpersonal animosity between the problem solvers interferes with their willingness and ability to deal with the substantive issues. It is an important first step to establish what kind(s) of issues there are.

Stage 2: Deal with Interpersonal Issues

Collaborative problem solving means that people have to be prepared to share their important needs and concerns, listen respectfully to the needs and concerns of others, and work together to reach a win-win solution. People who are involved in interpersonal conflict are unlikely to be willing and able to do this. Therefore if Stage 1 identifies important unresolved interpersonal issues, those should be dealt with first. Only when the parties are comfortable enough with one another and sufficient trust has been restored should they proceed to resolve substantive issues. In fact, we frequently find that once the interpersonal issues are addressed, the substantive issues become very easy to deal with.

Stage 3: Resolve Substantive Issues

People can concentrate on resolving substantive issues if no significant interpersonal conflicts are getting in the way. When this is the case, the parties can meet and follow a problem-solving process to arrive at solutions that take everyone's needs and ideas into account.

Now that we understand why the three stages are important, let us look at how they are carried out.

HOW TO DETERMINE UNDERLYING CAUSES

Sometimes the real causes are just what they seem to be; other times the real causes are not recognized or are disguised. For example, two professionals having a disagreement over how a service should be delivered may just have different perspectives and opinions about the best way to do things. Or one or both of them might suspect the motives of the other person in promoting a particular approach, perhaps for personal gain or out of malice. It is important to understand the real issues before trying to address them. The best way to do this is to talk to people in confidence.

Conduct Interviews

One-on-one interviews can provide the best insights into problems, as they are seen by the people they most affect. Private interviews work better than group interviews or focus groups because people are more likely to be honest and less likely to be influenced by their colleagues.

In order for people to speak honestly in an interview, they must feel safe. This means providing guarantees of confidentiality that people will trust. Sometimes they will accept these guarantees more readily from outsiders. You can tell a lot about the internal climate of the organization from the degree of suspicion that people exhibit.

Barbara: In the museum situation described earlier, we gave people written guarantees of confidentiality, backed up by a public statement by the CEO. We booked interview rooms in an area of the building that was remote from the department that people worked in. We provided an external number for people to use when scheduling interviews. Even so, people often walked by the interview room several times and would not enter until they had assured themselves that nobody was watching to see who entered. In another organization several people insisted on off-site interviews.

45

What people tell you in interviews may not be factual. Personal biases and subjective perceptions always color people's view of events. However, the analysis of all of the interviews will usually identify key issues that the group shares; if some people are mistaken or even dishonest, that usually becomes apparent. More often people simply have very different perspectives, and this variation may be part of the problem that needs to be addressed. Later, when the parties meet together, they will have an opportunity to clarify any areas of misunderstanding or explain the reasons for their different interpretations.

Identify and Categorize the Issues
A careful analysis of the results usually enables you to identify the key issues, as the people involved see them. These issues can usually be categorized as either interpersonal or substantive.

> *Sy:* In a residential care facility the key substantive issue was conflict between the nursing director and the residential director over the appropriate model for providing health care to the clients. Another substantive issue was widespread dissatisfaction among the staff over how meetings were run. These issues were overshadowed by interpersonal issues: an almost complete breakdown in communication between the two directors and between some of the staff reporting to them.

One way to decide whether a problem is largely interpersonal is to ask yourself whether resolving the particular substantive issues would likely reduce the level of tension between or among the parties. If you suspect they would still find a reason to fight, then you have an interpersonal issue that needs resolution.

HOW TO DEAL WITH
SIGNIFICANT INTERPERSONAL ISSUES

In order to collaborate on resolving substantive issues, people need to trust one another and communicate respectfully. Trust and communication do not have to be perfect in order for problem solving to proceed. However, if people are unwilling or unable to share information and ideas, collaboration will not work.

Help People Put Their Trust in the Process

Until the parties begin to trust each other, they need a secure process they can trust. Parties often feel more secure when they have an impartial and competent third party to help them keep the conversation constructive. They may also need other procedural safeguards (for example, confidentiality) to feel comfortable even sitting down with the other person. The process should help build trust between the parties by allowing parties to listen to each other and see other perspectives.

Explore Interpersonal Issues and Causes

During Stage 1 the interpersonal issues are identified. Now it is necessary to examine them more closely to find out their causes and origins. Are they caused by personality clashes, or lack of communication skills, or a past dispute that has been unresolved, or some combination of factors?

We use a variety of tools and techniques to uncover these causes and will discuss those in the sections that follow.

Personal Styles

There are some excellent and well-known instruments that can identify important (and not terribly sensitive) aspects of personal preferences. Examples are the Myers Briggs Type Instrument (MBTI) and the Hogan-Champagne Personal Style Inventory (1979). Both instruments measure four sets of preferences: introversion-extroversion, sensing-intuition, thinking-feeling, and judging-perceiving (see Figure 2.2, which is based on Briggs [1985]). Together they form sixteen different personal styles. None of the preferences or styles is better or worse than any others, but the styles are different, and these differences frequently lead to interpersonal conflict.

Barbara: A hospital Communication Disorders Department was made up of two professional sections: Audiology and Speech Pathology. One of the rub points in the department was the resentment the audiologists felt toward the speech pathologists and the director because of the "favoritism" shown by the director toward speech pathol-

Four Dimensions

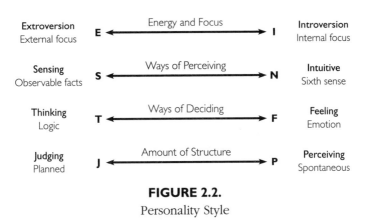

Extroversion External focus	E ←— Energy and Focus —→ I	Introversion Internal focus
Sensing Observable facts	S ←— Ways of Perceiving —→ N	Intuitive Sixth sense
Thinking Logic	T ←— Ways of Deciding —→ F	Feeling Emotion
Judging Planned	J ←— Amount of Structure —→ P	Perceiving Spontaneous

FIGURE 2.2.

Personality Style

ogy issues and the "self-centered" approach of the speech pathologists. According to the audiologists, department meetings focused almost exclusively on speech pathology's issues and concerns. Audiologists' issues were ignored, and their opinions were not sought. They had reached the stage of seeking secession or at least separate meetings.

The assessment instruments showed what we might have predicted: the audiologists were all strong introverts, whereas the speech pathologists were all strong extroverts, as was the director. Introverts tend to be quiet and thoughtful; extroverts communicate openly and like group problem solving. In joint meetings it was natural for the speech pathologists to raise and discuss their issues while the audiologists sat quietly and stewed. It was also natural for the speech pathologists and the director to assume that if the audiologists had anything to say they would say it.

Finding these things out did not make the problem go away, but it did provide a less blaming explanation than "favoritism" and being "self–centered."

Different Approaches to Dealing with Conflict

Earlier we explained the dual concern model of conflict resolution that identifies a person's predominant conflict mode: avoiding, competing, accommodating, compromising, and collaborating. Several instruments capture this information, one of which is the Thomas-Kilmann Conflict Mode Instrument (1974). The conflict modes of the parties to a conflict may explain at least some of the interpersonal friction.

Sy: Earlier in this chapter we described the serious conflict in a residential care facility caused by the almost complete breakdown in communication between the nursing director and the residential director and among some of the staff reporting to them. The animosities had reached the point where the executive director was concerned about the safety of the residents because critical decisions were not being made.

One of the issues between the directors was the nursing director's lack of trust. The nursing director told us that the two of them had typically met several days before meetings of the management committee in order to discuss agenda items and agree on a common position.

They would leave the meeting with an agreement, but increasingly the residential director would reverse herself at committee meetings, leaving the nursing director feeling betrayed. She was now refusing to meet with her colleague on the grounds that she was untrustworthy.

However, the residential director stated that the nursing director was aggressive and overpowering—pushing her into a corner on issues that required considerable thought. When she felt coerced, she said nothing, hoping to avoid an unpleasant confrontation. Also it was important to the residential director to consult her staff and, if possible, reflect the group's consensus on issues affecting them.

We asked the two directors and their staff to complete the Conflict Mode Instrument and the Personal Style Inventory. The nursing director turned out to be a competer and an extrovert. The residential director was an accommodator and an introvert. When we reviewed the results with them, the nature of the problem became clear to all of us. At the pre-meeting, the nursing director would put her ideas forward forcefully because that is what extroverted competers do. The residential director would listen quietly because that is what introverted accommodators do. At the end of the meeting the nursing director, having heard no counterarguments, would go away confident that they had reached agreement. However, the residential director, after reflecting on it for a few days and discussing it with her staff, would reach her own conclusions, which she would express at management committee meetings. Her position was frequently different from that expressed by the nursing director.

The point is that neither of these two people was acting in bad faith. They were just behaving according to their personal styles. The conflict arose because they did not understand each other's styles and therefore made assumptions about each other's motives.

Diverse Perceptions

Often people who have gotten on well together in the past experience an event that changes their relationship. They may perceive this event differently, and the different perceptions may contribute to subsequent conflict. We ask each person to describe the history of the relationship by drawing a curve on a chart and explaining the transitions (see Figure 2.3). The individual charts and the comparisons between them can be very illuminating.

> *Sy:* We were invited to intervene in a dispute between the editors of two separate but related journals in a publishing company. One of the editors had been with the company since its inception; the other had joined within the past year. The editor with longer service blamed the new person for her reduced morale and self-perceived loss of status in the organization. Their relationship quickly became conflicted, and the newer editor moved her office to a separate floor. The two editors refused to attend staff meetings together or to communicate directly. They constantly sniped at each other, and their colleagues were caught in the crossfire. Opportunities to

Name:

	3 Years ago	2 Years ago	1 Year ago	Today
Ideal working relationship				
Positive working relationship				
Neutral working relationship				
Negative working relationship				
Dysfunctional working relationship				

FIGURE 2.3.

Relationship History

capitalize on potential synergies were lost. The publisher was worried that the internal battles would become public and frighten away advertisers.

We asked each editor to complete a relationship history chart, and the first editor was shocked to discover that her anger and low morale had started at least six months before her counterpart arrived. When we pieced together the critical incidents, it turned out that she was angry with the publisher for restructuring the organization in a way that caused her to lose status. If the restructuring had not taken place, she would have become executive editor, and the new editor would have reported to her. She realized that she would have taken out her disappointment on anybody who moved into the new role, and it was not the new person's fault.

Discuss the Findings

We invite the parties to participate in a discussion of the assessment results, which we facilitate. Before discussing their particular results, we explain the instruments and the concepts behind them. During this explanation the parties frequently begin to interpret their own results and become interested in sharing results and discussing the implications. The resulting discussion usually enables the participants to understand the role played by personal approaches and perceptions and causes them to reconsider their previous assumptions about negative motivation.

Exchange Commitments

When the parties understand how the other party might have misinterpreted their behavior, they are usually willing to make commitments to reduce the negative consequences. These are confidence-building measures that allow them to work together to address the substantive issues. The parties can agree to implement these actions simultaneously, or one party can take the lead as an incentive to encourage reciprocal gestures. Just as actions can escalate tensions, gestures of goodwill can reverse the spiral and create optimism for problem solving.

> *Sy:* In the residential care facility the nursing director committed to check out her assumptions about whether or not

the residential director had agreed to a common approach or was just going to think about it. If it was the latter, the nursing director agreed to give her a few days to consider her position and consult her staff. In return the residential director promised to advise the nursing director of any decision she reached in advance of management committee meetings. They gave each other permission to remind them of their commitments.

RESOLVE THE SUBSTANTIVE ISSUES THROUGH AN INTEREST-BASED APPROACH

After Stage 2 has resolved the interpersonal issues (or after Stage 1 if there are no significant interpersonal issues), the parties are ready to work on the substantive disputes. The approach we use (see Figure 2.4) is derived from the Principled Negotiation Model developed by the Harvard Law School Program on Negotiation and described by Roger Fisher and William Ury in their book titled *Getting to Yes* (1991).

There are seven steps in the interest-based process we use. We'll discuss those in the sections that follow.

Step 1: Introduce the Process and Define the Issue

This is the opportunity for the manager, the facilitator, or one of the parties to lay the groundwork for everything that follows by making clear the objectives of the exercise, the

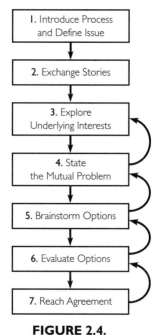

FIGURE 2.4.
Interest-Based Conflict Resolution

process to be followed, the ground rules, and so on. It is important to set a collaborative tone. The parties should be congratulated for agreeing to participate in a win-win process. They should be reminded that this is their opportunity to influence one another. These are some of the important items to cover.

The Issue to Be Addressed

What issue or issues will the parties address? What are the time, process, and resource constraints? In what order should they be discussed: easiest first or most urgent? Time should be taken to clarify these points and get understanding and agreement. Too often people rush into solutions before they have properly understood the nature and scope of the problem.

Best Alternative to a Negotiated Agreement

According to Fisher and Ury, each party in a dispute should understand his or her alternatives in the event that negotiations break down. They should determine the best, worst, and most likely alternatives to a negotiated agreement (known in the field collectively as BATNA). People should be informed of what will happen should they be unable to reach a decision, and they should be encouraged to think about the implications. If this is expressed appropriately, it may motivate members to take the process seriously. This reality check often makes the parties take the process seriously and increases their flexibility.

> *Sy:* In the conflict in the museum described in Chapter One, the two executives were resistant to meeting together to resolve their disagreements. In introducing us and our process, the CEO told them: "The situation between the two of you has become intolerable. It is affecting your staffs and has even disrupted the board. It cannot go on. I am giving you both the opportunity to be part of the solution of the problem by taking part in this collaborative

process. However, if you do not take this opportunity, I will take action myself, and neither of you may like my action."

The Process

The parties should understand the process, including the steps and the timetable. This will allow them to be patient and attentive by letting them know when they will have the chance to explain their positions, raise questions and objections, argue their points, and so on. People will have difficulty listening if they are concerned that their views will not be heard.

Ground Rules

The leader should establish the norms for the discussion. For example, people might be asked to refrain from interrupting each other, to make notes so that they can raise issues later, to speak respectfully, to not impute motives, and so on.

The issue of confidentiality should be discussed. All discussions should be kept confidential unless everyone agrees to disclose specific items. This invites people to be open in presenting ideas and information. The leader may have to clarify in advance with superiors or others any restrictions on confidentiality; these should be raised with the parties. If this is not done, senior people in management or unions may request and be given information that members of the team believe to be confidential. The result would be a loss of trust that could undermine the team and future teams.

Step 2: Exchange Stories

Each party to a dispute has a preferred outcome (position). The parties probably know enough about each other's positions to know that they are different, that is, they know why there is a conflict. This is their opportunity to state their positions clearly. Because the idea of interest-based negotiation is to get beyond positions and focus on interests, it is better to ask questions like, "What happened, from your perspective?" or "What do you hope to achieve?" rather than "What is your position?" This invites people to be less positional, even though most of the time you will hear their positions.

Step 3: Explore Underlying Interests

Participants should explain their needs, concerns, values, fears, and other interests underlying their positions. This allows the parties to better understand each other's positions; more important, it opens the door to new possibilities that satisfy the interests of all participants. If the position is thought of as the tip of the iceberg, the interests are the important material that is often hidden below the surface. During this step the parties are encouraged to assert and explain all of their interests. There are three types of interests: substantive, psychological, and procedural.

Substantive Interests

These are the tangible and most obvious interests that people are seeking. Disputants often explain the conflict according to these interests. For example, if asked what the fighting is about, disputants may say, "It's over money" or "We want more staff hired." Often people assume that these are the only interests at play, but other interests may be at least as important.

Psychological Interests

Everybody has psychological needs: the need to belong, to be respected, to get credit for achievements, to have losses acknowledged, and so on. These are less obvious than the substantive interests because we are reluctant to talk about them and may not even be conscious of them.

Procedural Interests

Sometimes the way a decision is reached may be important, possibly more important than the decision itself. For example, even though we strongly support a particular political party and have fundamental disagreements with the policies of another party, very few of us in the West would sacrifice free elections in order to keep our party in office. Our belief in democratic elections outweighs our distaste for the other party.

These types of interests can be proxies for one another. For example, if you won't acknowledge the embarrassment I experienced when you treated me badly (psychological), I will make you pay punitive monetary compensation (substantive). The effects of disregarding psychological or procedural interests may be negative for both parties. For example, you may end up making a larger financial settlement than necessary, and I may still feel dissatisfied because you did not apologize.

It is usual to find that, even when the parties have opposing positions, they have some important common interests, as well as other interests that are not in conflict. These noncompeting interests may foster a hopeful attitude and should be the basis for a collaborative resolution.

Step 4: Agree on a Mutual Problem Statement
The core concept of interest-based conflict resolution is to turn a conflict between parties into a problem that both parties are prepared to solve jointly. The Mutual Problem Statement is an umbrella statement that pulls together the most important interests of all parties. It often takes this form: How can we accomplish X while at the same time achieving Y and Z?

> *Sy:* In the museum described in Chapter One, the two key executives had very different visions for the organization, consistent with their own backgrounds and areas of responsibility. One visualized the museum as primarily an educational institution and therefore linked to the rest of the educational system. The other saw its primary goal as entertainment, competing for audiences with movies, theme parks, and the like.
>
> Instead of treating this as an either-or conflict (either an educational institution or an entertainment complex), it

was much more productive to work together on this as a both-and mutual problem: How can we create exhibits that entertain school and family audiences while at the same time educate those with a serious interest in the subject matter?

Step 5: Brainstorm Options for Solving the Mutual Problem Statement

Often the parties to a dispute can only visualize one workable option: the position each came in with. In addition to the substantive superiority of their positions, the parties have a psychological investment in them. If one party accepts the other party's position, there is also a loss of face.

In fact, there are usually several different ways to meet the parties' interests. If people can agree on a mutual problem statement, they can put their original positions on a back burner and brainstorm different ways to meet the underlying needs. If some of these new options meet the parties' interests as well as or even better than their original proposal, a resolution can be achieved without either party having to lose face.

The success of brainstorming depends on following several rules:

- The more options the better.

- Even "silly" options could prove valuable as a part of an overall solution.

- No comment or criticism about options can be made during brainstorming.

- Discussing an option does not mean accepting it.

- There will be an opportunity to discuss options when the brainstorming process is over.

Step 6: Evaluate Options
After all the ideas are out on the table, the parties can begin to clarify, debate, and evaluate them.

Participants should still use respectful communication in asking questions, answering them, and expressing reservations. Options should be explored fully, and efforts should be made to improve problematic ones before they are rejected.

Rarely do you get a complete solution from any one option. Incomplete options can be combined into complete packages. This process can produce a number of unexpected and creative alternatives.

A good way to evaluate options is to establish some objective criteria as a way of reducing the tendency to make subjective decisions. Those criteria might include

- How well do the options satisfy the Mutual Problem Statement (that is, the interests of the parties)?

- How costly are the options?

- How easily and quickly can the options be implemented?

- Are options legal and in line with company policy?

Step 7: Reach Agreement
The parties select the option that best satisfies the criteria. If the Mutual Problem Statement really reflects the key interests, and if the option generation is creative, the parties can often find a solution that is at least as good as either of their original positions. And it will meet with more acceptance.

The agreement should be spelled out clearly, preferably in writing. It should specify the responsibility for actions and the target dates. Unless this is done, conflict will arise based on different recollections and interpretations of the agreement.

A TRANSFORMATIONAL APPROACH
TO RESOLVING CONFLICT

In their landmark book *The Promise of Mediation* (1994), Robert A. Baruch Bush and Joseph P. Folger describe a transformational approach to resolving conflict. Rather than (or in addition to) settling specific disputes, followers of this approach set out to empower the parties to work together as problem solvers. The approach we described in this chapter does that. In the residential care facility, in the hospital Communication Disorders Department, and in the heavy-duty maintenance area, people began by viewing each other as untrustworthy adversaries and themselves as powerless to resolve the conflicts they were caught up in. At the end of the process, they saw each other as potential allies and had developed confidence in their joint ability to solve problems together. Several years later they were still collaborating, and some were good friends.

The process we follow would be well worth using on the basis of its ability to develop acceptable solutions to complex organizational conflicts and to transform relationships. It has another advantage as well: the solutions are not only acceptable but they are *creative*. In the next chapter we examine the creative aspect of our approach.

CHAPTER THREE

CREATIVE RESOLUTION OF CONFLICT

◯

While all firms face these conflicts, very, very few harness it productively. Like the twin perils of Scylla and Charybdis facing Odysseus on his homeward voyage, two ever-present dangers seem to consume most corporate efforts to handle contention. The first is "overdetermination" (taking a good thing too far), and the second is seeking the "golden mean"—a safe middle-of-the-road solution.

RICHARD TANNER PASCALE

In Chapter Two we described a collaborative approach to resolving organizational conflict. We explained how this approach usually results in high-quality solutions that the parties are committed to implement and at the same time builds strong long-term relationships. All of these benefits are important in supporting an effective organization and would be reason enough to promote this approach and train people to use it. However, we have found that the collaborative approach has another important benefit: *the solutions tend to be creative.* We believe that more attention should be paid to this result.

In this chapter we look at the importance of creativity in conflict resolution and examine the results of the collaborative process to see the extent to which they are creative. We also look at the factors that contribute to this creativity.

THE IMPORTANCE OF CREATIVITY IN CONFLICT RESOLUTION

What do we mean when we say that a solution to a problem is creative? Do we use an absolute standard of creativity in the way that Leonardo da Vinci was creative or Henry Ford or Alexander Graham Bell? They developed concepts or devices that had never been thought of or invented. But this seems too high to set the bar; the problems that most of us work on are much less dramatic and world changing. And few of us are geniuses. What standard, then, should we use?

It seems to us that we need a more relative standard—one that takes into account the nature of the problems and the capabilities of the problem solvers. In the context of conflict resolution we suggest that a solution should be considered creative if the parties were not aware of similar solutions to comparable conflicts.

Creativity is important in reaching the win-win resolution of conflicts. Parties in conflict usually see situations in black-white, win-lose terms. Each party enters the dispute resolution process with a firm position that represents his or her preferred resolution. Each party rejects the other's position (or there would be no conflict). To accept the other party's position would be to give in—to lose. The usual (and uncreative) way of resolving conflicts is through compromise, that is, narrowing the gap between the opposing positions until an acceptable compromise is reached. Thus neither party has fully lost nor fully won, and both are partly satisfied. Of course both are also partly unsatisfied. It is not unusual for both parties to a compromise agreement to walk away feeling somewhat empty and unfulfilled.

Collaboration opens the door to win-win solutions by *creating new options,* often different from either position, and even different from any solution the parties might be able to imagine at the beginning of the process. The fact that these new options do not belong to either party allows both sides to consider them wins rather than losses.

Collaboration does not always result in creative solutions. Sometimes the best that can be accomplished is a compromise. However, in an impressive proportion of situations the results are truly creative. Sometimes the creativity is reflected in a small but crucial component of the solution that makes the rest of it acceptable; sometimes the whole solution is dramatically creative.

Let us examine some collaborative solutions in terms of creativity.

EXAMPLES OF CREATIVE SOLUTIONS

Our work with a variety of organizations has yielded many examples of unexpected and creative outcomes, some of which we now describe.

> *Sy:* In the residential treatment center described in Chapter Two the nursing director and the residential director were in disagreement over the appropriate model for providing health care to the clients, most of whom had serious and complex medical conditions. The nursing director advocated a centralized model in which the specially trained nurses and doctors at the head office would make decisions about health care; they would also treat the residents. The residential director favored a community-based model. In the interest of providing a homelike environment and convenient medical care, she believed that the residential coordinator at each home should make decisions about when and where to seek treatment for residents.
>
> After resolving the interpersonal conflict between them, the two directors and the rest of the management team

met to address the issue of providing health care. Their solution was to use a community-based model but one in which the specialized health care professionals would offer on-site treatment of high-risk conditions and would approve local doctors for more routine problems following special in-service training. Nursing assistants would be assigned to join the teams at the residences to help with daily health care decisions, and nursing specialists would be available for consultation on more complex issues.

The solution they reached was a good one, and all participants supported it. (This would not have been the case with either of the initial proposals.) Was it also creative?

We do not know whether other, similar facilities have developed similar models. Given that there are thousands of such facilities, we expect that this solution is not unique. However, we would argue that it *is* creative. First of all it was not the approach being used by this institution at this time. Second, neither director proposed such an approach initially, and at the beginning of management discussions nobody else did either. The general assumption was that one of the two competing proposals would probably be selected, possibly with a few modifications.

After a collaborative problem-solving process, people agreed on a solution that was different from the existing approach and from any of the proposals. This solution met all of the concerns that each had raised and was uniquely appropriate for their facility. We believe that this qualifies as a creative solution. It was certainly more creative than any of the key players would have developed on her own.

> *Sy:* We were mediating a marriage breakdown between a husband and wife who were also business partners. The disposition of the family business was a major area of contention. Both agreed that, for various reasons, he should end up with the business, but they disagreed strongly about the amount of the buyout.
>
> He argued that the business was worth $500,000, and therefore her share was $250,000. She wanted $600,000 for her share of the business on the grounds that their past five years of joint effort were just on the verge of paying off. She believed that the next few years would show dramatic profit growth, and she resented not being able to share in it.
>
> The most obvious approach was to retain a business valuator to assess the business. This would be expensive because of the unusual nature of the business, and whatever value would eventually be assigned would leave one of them very unhappy. We helped them through a collaborative process that resulted in the following agreement. He would buy her shares in the company for $250,000 up front. In addition she would receive 25 percent of the increase in profits over the next five years (reflecting the five years she had already put into the business). This solution not only satisfied her financial needs but it met her psychological need to realize the

rewards of her contribution. The benefit for him was that it made his financial payment possible and set a definite termination date for their business relationship.

Was this a creative solution? We think so. Neither of the parties nor their lawyers had thought of this solution until it came up during our mediation session. Nor were they (or we) aware of similar arrangements elsewhere. No doubt, similar arrangements do exist, but that does not diminish the creativity inspired by the collaborative process.

Barbara: I facilitated a dispute between two companies that had had a long and valued business relationship. The companies had their headquarters in different cities. One firm was primarily in the consulting business, and the other was mainly in the management training business, but they each provided some overlapping services. Several years before, they had entered into an agreement to market one another's products and services but not to compete in each other's home city. This arrangement had worked to the benefit of both companies for many years.

A few months before I was called in, the training company learned that the consulting firm had won a large contract to do both consulting and training across the country in all of the cities where a major client had offices. This included the home city of the training company. Nothing had been discussed in advance, and the training company felt betrayed. It stopped employing the consulting firm in its training programs, and when its annual catalog was printed, the consulting firm was no longer mentioned. This action left the consulting firm feeling equally betrayed. Both parties were thinking of terminating their relationship and suing for breach of contract.

In the mediation it became clear that, without any evil intentions, both companies had gradually expanded to include many of the same types of services, and the two areas of training and consulting were beginning to merge. Because both dealt with national and multinational clients, the geographic noncompetition clause didn't work.

Once the issue of betrayal of trust was resolved, we followed an interest-based process to resolve the conflict. We agreed to consider all options, including ending their business relationship. Both parties wanted to be sure that any result would preserve a feeling of goodwill.

The solution they reached included replacing the geographic noncompetition agreement with one that dealt with the type of service: one company would manage all of the training contracts nationwide for both companies, and the other would manage the consulting services for both companies nationwide. The two CEOs agreed to communicate about all new contracts so that overlapping contracts could be allocated in a fair and equitable way.

They also agreed to take steps toward a possible merger but would maintain their autonomy until the whole agreement was reviewed in three years. At that time they would decide, based on criteria we worked out, whether to merge or to go their separate ways.

But was this creative? The solution was certainly very different from their initial positions. In fact, it was diametrically opposite from anything either firm had even considered. As a result of clarifying their motives, exploring each other's interests, and brainstorming a full range of interest-based options, they moved from ending their relationship and contemplating law suits to a new partnership and possible merger.

Barbara: I was mediating a case of a couple on a native reserve who were ending both their marriage and their family business. In this case the wife (who was non-native) really wanted to continue the business; it was the only work she felt she had been trained for, and the business was central to her life. The husband was far less involved in the business and would have been happy to be bought out, but this obvious solution was not possible for two reasons. First, in this jurisdiction non-natives cannot run businesses on reserves and enjoy the same tax benefits as native-run businesses. Second, the husband's family objected to the loss of a business that had a long and proud history. The wife's alternative plan was to start a similar business close to the reserve, but the husband was concerned that this would threaten his livelihood. Soon the parties were in an adversarial mode, each accusing the other of bad faith and sabotage.

It was necessary to rebuild the trust between them and help them recognize that she would not want to undermine the business she had invested so much effort in, and he did not want to keep her in a dependent position forever. The solution they reached was that he offered to pay her a declining percentage of the family business revenues over a minimum of five years in return for a minimum of two years when she would not compete. In return he would pay for her to complete a university degree she had stopped pursuing when they married. This degree would prepare her for work in a related field that would use her accumulated expertise but not undermine the family business. Also he agreed that the family business would be passed on to their oldest child, who already worked in the business and had a close relationship with the mother. The agreement would be reviewed at the end of five years to see if she continued to need support to supplement her income. The particular terms of this agreement allowed for growth and change for both parties and included incentives or safeguards to ensure that the spirit of the agreement was carried out.

Again the solution was creative in that it was different from anything the parties had even imagined prior to entering the process.

Barbara: I was mediating an estate case involving two sisters. In addition to the parties there were three lawyers and an executor; all were fighting over the disposition of the parents' home and household possessions. When they came to see me, the only plan was to sell the home and contents on a power of sale and split the proceeds if any were left after legal fees.

When I asked about their respective interests in their parents' home, it immediately became clear that they wanted very different things. One sister, who lived and worked in another city, wanted to sell the home in order to raise the down payment for a home of her own. The other sister was unable to work due to a physical handicap. She needed a roof over her head and wanted to live in this house for sentimental reasons. She wanted to achieve some feeling of closeness with her parents and redress what she saw as their favoritism of her sister.

The solution we reached on the disposition of the home was that one sister would buy out the other at a fair market price. We resolved the conflict over the household contents by listing all the items and having each sister rank each item by importance. After each sister had an opportunity to explain why the items were important, the overlap was reduced to four items (out of an initial three-page list). The eventual result was that, out of an entire household of items, each sister got all but two of her most important items.

An excellent example of the creative potential of collaborative negotiation happened in the British Columbia logging dispute.

The area of Clayoquot Sound, home of old-growth rainforest, became a battleground in the early 1990s, pitting logging companies and their workers against environmentalists and First Nations (aboriginal) communities. Eight hundred people were arrested in the biggest show of civil disobedience in Canadian history.

After years of acrimony and impasse, parties on all sides of the dispute agreed to join peace talks. They used a collaborative negotiation approach to find some way to meet their very different interests. The end result of two years of talks was the creation of a new forestry company that would operate very differently from other logging companies. There would be no more clear-cutting, only selective harvesting. The environmentalists would help promote the wood as environmentally friendly so that it could be sold at a premium both domestically and internationally. The company would be owned 51 percent by local First Nations and 49 percent by forestry giant Weyerhaeuser; First Nations communities would get forestry jobs from the company. In this way an unprecedented dispute became an unprecedented solution.

We have observed over and over that parties to a conflict who follow a collaborative dispute resolution process often come up with agreements that are more creative than they would have reached through other means. Let us explore the factors that contribute to this creativity.

FACTORS CONTRIBUTING TO
CREATIVE CONFLICT RESOLUTION

What is required to achieve the paradigm shift from attacking each other to solving the problem collaboratively and creatively? The following are several factors that are important to unlock the creative potential.

The Conflict Is Reframed as a Problem

Conflict invites opposition. People generally view the resolution of a conflict as being an either-or proposition: either one party wins, or the other one does. All the creative energy goes into outdoing each other.

But problem solving can be viewed as a both-and proposition: How can we reach a solution that meets all of the important needs of both (all) parties? Problem solving invites integration and synergy and directs the creative energy to that end.

People feel a lot more creative when they see themselves working on a problem with colleagues than when they are resolving conflicts with adversaries. An interest-based process redefines the conflict between the parties as a problem to be solved jointly through their combined experience and perspective. This redefinition is neither a fictional construct nor an attempt to gloss over differences. It is an attempt to redirect people's energies from attacking each other to working on the same side of the table and attacking the problem.

79

This approach requires some safeguards for parties that are initially distrustful, but the rewards for shifting from competition to collaboration can be considerable. First, if parties are collaborators rather than competitors, they can share information much more freely. It is difficult to solve any complex problem if relevant information isn't shared. Second, efforts directed at undermining or criticizing the other party can be shifted to exploring how objectives can be met that are important to all sides. Third, when cooperation replaces competition, results can often be achieved in a more efficient and cost-effective manner. Fourth, the synergy of working together produces surprisingly creative results.

In our experience a conflict is just a problem that needs solving, but the solution is made difficult because the parties have become committed to opposing positions. An interest-based process like ours helps them step back and become uncommitted to their specific positions and then move on to problem solving.

Trust Promotes Risk Taking
Creativity requires people to take risks, including the risk of voicing unusual and unpopular opinions with the added possibility of looking foolish. Accepting the risk of considering ideas that seem counterintuitive is another prerequisite of creativity.

Adversarial conditions discourage risk taking. The well-worn adages, "Keep your cards close to your chest" and "Don't tell the other person anything that he or she doesn't already know," are negotiating strategies born out of distrust. They suggest the need for being guarded and protecting your turf (in this case your knowledge, ideas, and experience). This is the opposite of what is needed to work creatively with others.

Our process helps people trust one another by setting a collaborative tone and by first repairing damaged interpersonal relationships before addressing the substantive issues. Once people feel heard and understood and have overcome their personal animosities, they are more prepared to cooperate.

Two Heads Are Better Than One When Solving Problems

When faced with difficult problems, most of us would benefit from consultation with other knowledgeable people. This is especially true if those people have different experiences and knowledge and yet share common interests in achieving organizational goals.

Very often the colleagues with whom we are in conflict would be the best people to consult with, if we could see that objectively. They understand the organization and the situation better than most outsiders would. They have experience, knowledge, and perspectives that are different from ours, yet not too different, and are probably as committed to the organization's goals as we are. If they buy into the solution of the problem, they can help implement it—something that outside consultants usually cannot do.

You Can Be More Creative with Interests Than with Positions

Positions are people's preferred solutions to problems. They represent what individuals working alone, often with a competitive mentality, think will best meet their own needs. These positions often become entrenched, leaving little room for creative thinking.

Interests are more conducive to creative thinking than positions are. Interests do not represent solutions but do represent the important needs that must be met through whatever solution is reached. If the parties focus on their interests while suspending their positions, they can brainstorm many creative options that meet their underlying needs and select the best solution.

The Structured Process Provides Time for Creativity

Most people find conflict and conflict resolution to be uncomfortable, so they usually try to rush to solutions. We have observed a strong tendency for parties to start constructing an agreement before they have completely understood the real issues. Such agreements are rarely creative.

Creativity is hard work. People in conflict cannot develop innovative solutions quickly. They need time to fully understand the issues, to repair relationships, to explore each other's interests, to share information, and to generate and consider options. In brainstorming the most creative ideas are rarely the first ones proposed. Following a structured process slows down the problem solving so that creativity can occur.

Suspending Judgment Enhances Brainstorming

In brainstorming, the free-flow generation of options (right-brain imagination) is separated from the evaluation of the ideas (left-brain judgment). This is an important factor in encouraging parties to suggest more options because criticizing or even commenting on options interferes with brainstorming. Our experience and that of many other facilitators is that the more options generated during brainstorming, the better and more creative are the agreements reached.

We encourage people to propose options without regard for their practicality and insist that they suspend judgment about any options until brainstorming is finished. We find that even some of the more far-fetched options frequently become essential components of successful solutions.

Evaluation Using Objective Criteria Helps Brainstorming

Objective criteria and an insistence on accurate information pushes parties to research their problem in greater depth. On the face of it "objective criteria," "accurate information," and "research" seem to be inimical to creativity. In our experience this is not the case. Careful analysis helps define the problem, and knowing that options will be examined carefully against objective criteria reassures people enough to permit them to suspend judgment during brainstorming.

Awareness of BATNA Promotes Acceptance of New Ideas

In the interest-based process people are encouraged to think about their alternatives in the event that negotiations break down. Very often these alternatives are not attractive. When the going gets tough, people with unappealing BATNAs often become more receptive to new ideas. If necessity is the mother of invention, a poor BATNA might be its father.

Experienced interest-based mediators are well aware of the creative nature of collaborative dispute resolution. We ourselves have often been dazzled by innovative solutions that neither the parties nor the mediators could have foreseen. This has led us to ask the question: If parties in conflict can work together to develop creative solutions, can a similar process be used as a vehicle for creative problem solving, even where there is no preexisting conflict? This will be the subject of Part Two of the book.

PART TWO

Enhancing Creativity Through Conflict

CHAPTER FOUR

CONFLICT: THE OXYGEN OF CREATIVITY?

An idea grows by annexing its neighbors.

ERNEST DIMNET

Part One of this book looked at destructive conflict and how an interest-based approach could enable adversaries to produce creative solutions from such conflict. Now in Part Two we address this question: Can conflict, properly managed, be an engine for creativity? And can a similar interest-based process produce creative solutions where there is no destructive conflict and where the parties are not adversaries? Before we address those questions, let us examine some of the dilemmas that organizations face when trying to foster creativity in their people.

THE CREATIVE IMPERATIVE

As recently as one or two generations ago you could spend your entire working life performing the same tasks in essentially the same way in the same organization. Most of your job was repetitive. In fact, the things that made you increasingly valuable were the expertise you had developed through repetition and the factual information you carried in your head. By and large you were not expected to deal with unusual situations; these were referred upward to your boss or to a specially trained professional.

Even the early years of computers did not really change this pattern. Computers simply provided a tool to make workers more efficient at their usual tasks.

> *Sy:* In the mid-1960s I was a business systems analyst for a *Fortune* 500 company. My role was to research the way tasks were performed in order to insert computers into the process with minimum disruption. After retraining, the same people continued to do work that was similar to what they had done previously but with more efficient tools. I was surprised to find, almost thirty years later, that at least one of the systems I designed in the sixties was still in use. (In my own small way I thus contributed to the Y2K scare.)

Today's world is changing rapidly and unpredictably. Experienced people and well-documented procedures are far less helpful. What is the value of people who have intimate knowledge of processes that no longer exist? Or what about those who have accumulated encyclopedic knowledge through years of experience that can now be accessed in seconds from a computer database by a relative newcomer? Unless they are able and willing to adapt quickly and continuously, these people may actually be detrimental to the organization because they respond to new challenges in ways that are no longer relevant.

Take the stock market, for example. For years the effectiveness of the stock market depended on having experienced analysts, brokers, floor traders, back room accountants, and so on. The trading of stocks changed little from one generation to the next. It is true that efficiencies resulted from technology and mergers, but the market was essentially the same.

Could a Rip van Winkle, asleep since the 1960s, recognize the stock market today? It is increasingly a virtual industry, as more and more people carry out their own trading via the Internet. Floor traders have all but disappeared. The back room is mostly automated. Information that used to be provided by salesmen is now available on the World Wide Web. Experience is still valuable but mainly because it helps identify the pieces of the growing information pile that are the most important and understand their implications.

What is true in the stock market is true almost everywhere. Organizations depend increasingly on problem solvers, that is, people who not only have the skills and knowledge to innovate but who love the challenge of doing so. But individual creativity and problem solving may not be enough. In fact, creative individuals have limited impact in organizations.

THE IMPACT OF CREATIVE INDIVIDUALS

Several factors combine to reduce the effect of creative individuals on organizations. We'll discuss these in the sections that follow.

Factor 1: Too Few Creative People in Organizations

Creativity is the ability to come up with unconventional responses to problems and opportunities. To be creative you must be able and willing to generate and consider options that are new and unusual. There may be countless creative people in the world, but many of them do not adapt well to structured environments like corporations, institutions, or governments. The very thought processes that foster creativity make those people unwilling or unable to work within organizational structures.

Factor 2: Problems too Complex for One Individual

Even if you disagree with our view of the scarcity of creative people in organizations, you might still agree that individual creativity has limited impact. Creativity is potential energy; it must be applied to a body of knowledge in order to generate useful ideas. Complex issues require broad and varied information. Today's challenges require more information, more ideas, and more support than any single individual can possess, no matter how intelligent and experienced.

There are several ironies here. One is that at the same time the explosion of knowledge makes it necessary for more of us to become increasingly specialized in narrower fields, organizational success depends on an interdisciplinary and systemwide perspective. Another irony is that it takes many years to accumulate the required depth and breadth of experience, and people who have worked in a field for that long tend to resist innovation.

Factor 3: Hindrance of Risk Taking by Organizational Rules
A concept that is related to creativity and often subsumed within it is innovation: the practical application of new ideas or the novel application of existing ideas. In fact, creativity is of no use to society without innovation, which depends on creativity but adds to it the need for taking risks.

Most people who work in organizations are not risk takers. Despite claims made by organizations that failures are valued as learning experiences, most of us have seen or experienced the opposite. People are generally punished for failure, and in most organizations the cost of failure outweighs the benefits of success. Even if individuals are willing to take risks, most organizations have bureaucratic processes to restrict risk taking.

Factor 4: Difficulty Selling New Ideas to Decision Makers

It is very difficult for any individual to introduce a new idea to a corporation for many reasons. First, people tend to resist new ideas, especially those developed by someone else. Second, it is hard for one person from one work area to understand the implications of the ideas on people in other areas and to be aware of the "hot buttons" that will be persuasive to them. Third, creative individuals may be even less persuasive because they may be perceived as being antagonistic to the norms of the organization.

Factor 5: Lack of Critical Mass of Committed People to Carry Out New Ideas

Even after permission has been granted to implement a new idea, resistance should be anticipated. The more people who are motivated to carry forward the implementation in the face of this resistance the more successful it will be. Ideas developed by individuals are unlikely to have enough champions.

If creative individuals are not the answer to organizational success, what about creative groups or teams?

THE IMPACT OF CREATIVE GROUPS

"Thinking is a social activity," says philosopher Michael Ignatieff (2000). Ignatieff says that we tend to think of new ideas as the product of solitary individuals, but history shows otherwise. He finds that most of the philosophical shifts of history were the product of groups who existed within a creative culture. We believe that the same can be said of innovation in organizations. In our work in organizational conflict resolution and group facilitation, we have been impressed with the creative powers of groups of people.

Many leaders have recognized that teams have a greater impact on organizational change than do individuals. Organizations of all kinds use teams or groups to improve internal systems, develop strategic plans, and address complex challenges. One of the most popular early uses of groups to solve problems creatively was "quality circles"—small groups of employees who meet periodically to solve problems relating to productivity and quality.

3M is a company renowned for its innovation. 3M's definition of *innovation* emphasizes both the conception and the implementation of a new idea. 3M finds that "several key skills may be found in one person—the so-called *inventorpreneur*—but increasingly they reside in a cross-functional team or a whole business unit" (Gundling, 2000, p. 188).

In terms of organizational creativity, groups have a greater potential impact than even highly creative individuals for several reasons, which we discuss next.

Greater Collective Knowledge of Group Members
Knowledge is the raw material of creativity. A group made up of people with different training and experience will start from a better knowledge base than that of any of them individually.

Generation of More Ideas by a Group
The more people there are, the more ideas are possible. And one person's ideas usually stimulate the thought process of the others, often leading to ideas that are different from any the individuals in the group could have generated alone. Alex Osborn, who developed the process of brainstorming in 1957 to increase the creativity of the employees in his advertising firm, did so in the expectation that "chain reactions" would occur that would allow a group to surpass the creativity of an individual. This phenomenon is well known to anyone who has participated in a well-run brainstorming exercise.

More People to Champion New Ideas
Several people representing different areas of the organization and different professional fields can usually have more influence in selling ideas across the organization than a single individual. They have more contacts and more persuasive arguments.

More People Committed to Implementing Group Decisions

One of the major challenges in trying to implement new ideas is to find enough people who understand the change and are dedicated to moving forward. Creative ideas developed by a group of people already have several committed change agents.

Sy: When I was first appointed to head up Human Resources, I was looking for ways to introduce people management innovations to the corporation. I wanted to have maximum impact, but I was concerned that there would be resistance at senior levels for several reasons. First, I was relatively new to a company that valued long service, and I would be seen as not understanding the organizational culture. Second, the HR division had acquired a reputation for flakiness, and its proposals tended to be discounted. Third, although I was confident in my department's creative powers, I was not confident in our understanding of the needs of the operating areas of the company.

I identified executive colleagues of mine across the company who were well respected and who seemed to share some of the key values of the HR Department. I invited them to join a just-formed corporate HR committee, and most of them agreed. These executives had perspectives that differed from mine and from each other's. They certainly were not prepared to rubber-stamp HR's proposals. Debates were vigorous and often contentious, and it sometimes took several meetings to work out the differences. However, over the next few years the committee generated proposals for creative management policies and practices, many of which were approved by senior management and were successfully implemented. The company became known as having the most creative HR practices in our industry. I attribute this success to the participation of such a broad group of experienced executives who understood the culture of the company and their own areas and who were politically connected.

Barbara: I was facilitating a very sensitive initiative to come up with a code of conduct for family mediators that would reflect concerns about power imbalances and domestic violence. Several stakeholder groups were suspicious of mediation. In fact, there had been some successful efforts to lobby governments against family mediation. It was clear that any policy developed by mediators alone would be unacceptable, and no opposing group on its own would "break ranks" to work with mediators.

Although the level of mistrust between the various groups was high, all cared deeply about the issue. We arranged a series of meetings involving all stakeholder groups. After listening respectfully to each other's concerns and views, the participants gained a deeper understanding of the issues; they jointly developed a far more appropriate and creative set of standards of professional conduct in cases of abuse. This code shifted thinking in the mediation field in a powerful way and built bridges of understanding between the diverse groups.

Why were the groups in these two examples creative? Certainly the four factors listed earlier contributed. However, we think a fifth factor played an important part.

The Superior Solutions That Result
from a Competition of Ideas

Several people can strengthen ideas by challenging them and by adding new information. They can also expose the flaws in unrealistic ideas. Thus the solutions are more likely to be innovative—able to be implemented—as well as creative.

In both the HR committee and family mediator examples the tension between the participants led to more energetic debate than would have taken place had everyone started on the same side of the table. In our view conflict contributed significantly to the creative outcomes.

CONFLICT AND CREATIVITY

The link between conflict and creativity is by no means new, but it is often overlooked. Hegelian philosophy advanced the notion that a new idea emerges as the *synthesis* of a battle between a *thesis* and an *antithesis*. In the business world many corporations have used similar concepts to foster creativity. Procter & Gamble, for example, has had a policy of "creative conflict" since 1931, encouraging competition among its various brands (Peters and Waterman, 1982). J. Hirshberg (1998), head of Nissan Design International, harnessed the "creative abrasion" of diverse individuals to stimulate debate over new car models. In their landmark book, Peters and Waterman observed that in innovative companies (such as Exxon and Citibank) meetings were far from polite affairs:

> The difference between their behavior and that of their competitors is nothing short of astonishing. They make a presentation, and then the screaming and shouting begin. The questions are unabashed; the flow is free; everyone is involved. Nobody hesitates to cut off the chairman, the president, a board member [p. 219].

Whether or not you agree that impolite behavior is an essential component of creativity, it seems clear that these corporations, among many others, believe that contention fosters creativity. This has been our experience as well.

Sy: I had an opportunity to observe firsthand the difference in creativity between two similar groups, one that valued conflict and one that did not. When I was an HR executive, I often took part in executive committee meetings. At our company, conflict was part of the culture, and it was acceptable to challenge vociferously other people's ideas. Executive decisions were frequently reached only after loud and contentious debates, similar to the Exxon and Citibank meetings described. Nothing was off-limits. Executives felt free to disagree openly with decisions made by other executives in their own divisions. As a result of this, meetings were rarely pleasant, but they were creative. We were known in our industry as being innovative and somewhat off-the-wall.

Several years later I consulted to a competitor organization. Their approach was more refined. Executives tended to mind their own business rather than debate issues at the executive committee. More decisions were made individually or through a series of one-on-one discussions. The company was not known for its creativity. (Things changed after an executive from my former company joined the competitor!)

As we have shown, there are many examples of creative groups, and constructive conflict within the group can foster increased creativity. Of course, not all groups are equally creative, and some are not creative at all. What determines the extent of group creativity?

Many factors contribute, including the size of a group, the creativity of individual members, the personalities and communication styles of the members, the relationships among members, the facilitation skills of the group leader, and the problem-solving process being used. However, in our experience the most important factor is *diversity*. Groups made up of people with different cultural and educational backgrounds, different personalities, different professional backgrounds, and different skills are potentially more creative and innovative than relatively homogenous groups. Their potential creativity can be realized through participation in a process that encourages the sharing of their diverse experiences.

WHY DIVERSITY IS AN ADVANTAGE

For many years the increasing diversity in society was not reflected in our organizations, which continued to be primarily white, Northern European, and male in all but the most menial supporting roles. Even women, who comprised over 50 percent of the population, were ignored for meaningful jobs. Everyone dressed the same, adhered to strict norms of conduct, and generally tried to avoid rocking the boat. Today's organizations are more visibly diverse and probably more open to such diversity than a generation ago.

Once organizations were forced into diversity, they found that variety has important advantages:

- Diverse workplaces are more interesting.

- Workplaces whose members reflect the broader community are better able to understand and meet the needs of diverse potential customers.

- Diversity brings with it a variety of opinions and ideas that enhance creativity.

In contrast to diverse groups, more homogenous groups tend to be less creative problem solvers. In fact, group dynamics can make homogenous groups far less effective than either single individuals or diverse groups. Groupthink, a dynamic identified by Irving Janis (1972), is one of the great dangers of homogenous groups. When group members share similar backgrounds and ideologies, cohesion within the group can be quite strong. If loyalty to the group becomes too strong, members will quickly agree to decisions that the rest of the group seems to support. As Janis states, the unspoken norm in groupthink is, "Preserve group harmony by going along uncritically with whatever consensus seems to be emerging" (1989, p. 57). The effects are reflected in poor decisions and low creativity.

Janis found groupthink to be responsible for foreign policy fiascoes like the Kennedy administration's Bay of Pigs invasion and the Nixon administration's decision to cover up the Watergate break-in. In both cases a handful of people who shared very similar ideological views were isolated from any outside review of their decisions and were discouraged from voicing any dissenting opinions. Those people made decisions that had disastrous outcomes.

In his book *The Abilene Paradox* (1996), Jerry B. Harvey tells the story of a son who returns with his new wife to visit his parents in rural Texas. While sitting around sipping lemonade on a very hot and dusty day, they all accept the father's suggestion that they drive more than one hundred miles to Abilene for dinner. When they return home after an exhausting and unpleasant trip, it turns out that none of them, including Dad, actually wanted to drive to Abilene. He had made the offer out of a mistaken belief that the newlyweds were bored, and the rest agreed because they did not want to disappoint one another. The story has served as a powerful illustration of how a group can make a poor decision that meets no one's interests despite (or rather because of) the desire to please others in the group.

Barbara: I was on a board of directors that decided to hold its annual Fall conference in Toronto. The leaders on the board were enthusiastically promoting the conference as the best way to increase membership and generate revenues. When a board member pointed out that another organization was well under way in organizing a conference in Toronto within a few weeks of our own, the majority decided to ignore this information; they rejected the idea of proposing a joint conference. Group solidarity was preserved, but our conference eventually had to be canceled and ended up a money loser rather than a money maker.

DESTRUCTIVE CONFLICT

Diversity is at the same time a reality, a blessing, and a curse. It is a reality because North American society is highly disparate in religion, race, culture, and language and is becoming more so. It is a blessing because diversity enriches our lives and fosters creativity. It is a curse because our intolerance of differences breeds conflict.

We have suggested that diversity has many *potential* advantages. This potential may not always be realized. Most of us have been part of diverse groups that *failed* to identify important opportunities and challenges, did *not* generate creative options, and did *not* make practical decisions that were widely accepted and successfully implemented. In fact, some of us have been on teams that blew apart in dissention and produced majority and minority recommendations.

> *Sy:* Several years ago the Canadian federal government established a Royal Commission to look into some important health issues. It appointed a very diverse group of members with the obvious expectation that this variety would lead to creative and innovative recommendations.
> Instead, the commission became bogged down in infighting and threatened lawsuits among its members and produced several minority reports.

> *Daryl:* During my graduate studies in conflict resolution, a group of students formed to confront concerns of political correctness, racism, and alienated groups in our department—in other words, diversity issues. This group of students of varying personal and cultural backgrounds met several times to analyze and develop a strategy to tackle these difficult problems. Nothing came of our efforts because the group splintered along gender, racial,

103

and professional lines. Members disagreed on several issues, including how the group should be run (leadership, agendas, time lines), what the nature of the problems were (primarily racism or primarily political correctness), and how they should be addressed (at the interpersonal or the systemic level). It became apparent that our different life experiences made us look at problems and solutions in very different ways. Sometimes we simply did not understand each other. Looking back, it is obvious that our very diversity was an obstacle to addressing issues related to diversity.

Because of the risks of dissention, some authors have cautioned against leaping into the current trend of cross-functional and diverse teams. Other writers support increased diversity on teams but still point out potential dangers. Taylor Cox Jr., for instance, says that the "value-in-diversity" philosophy is potentially correct, but diversity can have negative effects on communication and teamwork (1993, p. 17). John P. Fernandez, author of *The Diversity Advantage* (1993), says that organizations must deal effectively with the conflicts that result from a diverse workforce or risk losing the advantages of teamwork. As our examples illustrate, dialogue among disparate people is very difficult and is complicated by differences in values and experience. Such differences can quickly lead to a loss of respect and trust, as well as an increase in negative conflict.

We are faced with a dilemma. Diversity is important for innovation, but it is also a prime ingredient for potentially destructive conflict. An analogy can be made to chemistry. Two chemical substances that are kept separate may do little, but brought together they combine and react to produce something quite new and energetic. Yet the results of the reaction can be unpredictable and even explosive if they are not properly controlled.

THE DIVERSITY DILEMMA

Recall that in Chapter One we defined *conflict* as the product of diversity and interdependence. When people with different ideas and goals have to work together, you will get conflict. In order to reduce conflict, you would have to either reduce the diversity among people working together (to achieve harmony) or reduce the amount of teamwork and interaction (in favor of autonomy) (see Figure 4.1). In today's work environment neither of these approaches is feasible or even desirable because either would impair creativity.

Organizations must manage diversity in such a way as to maximize its advantages and minimize its disadvantages. If the potential advantages of diverse groups are to be realized, members must be willing and able to express and debate competing ideas vigorously yet be ready to join in implementing decisions that may differ from their own preferred options.

105

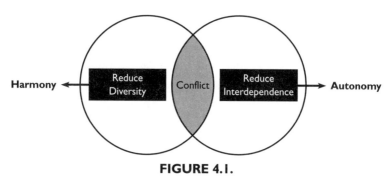

FIGURE 4.1.

Typical Approaches for Reducing Conflict

Richard Tanner Pascale (1990) conducted an excellent study of innovative companies and found that they embrace paradox and tension. He points to Honda as an illustration of a company with "a contention-management system that facilitates, rather than suppresses, conflict" (p. 26). Honda is a very decentralized corporation and has conflict between its separate companies and departments. Therefore it decided to manage this contention in a constructive way.

One approach Honda used is w*aigaya* (why-guy-ya)—a Japanese word connoting the noise of debate. The company holds regular meetings in which subordinates are invited to openly, though politely, challenge their bosses. Honda's cofounder, Takeo Fujisawa, explained to Pascale in an interview that fostering such open debate is similar to conducting an orchestra: "As president, you must orchestrate the discordant sounds into a kind of harmony. But you never want too much harmony. One must cultivate a taste for finding harmony within discord, or you will drift away from the forces that keep a company alive" (p. 256). With *waigaya,* it is the communication skills of the participants and the facilitator that keep the meetings from degenerating into gripe sessions.

Honda also employs cross-functional teams. The teams are often composed of young and new employees who have the right blend of personality and knowledge and are likely to see the problem in an unorthodox way.

This spirit of debate and questioning contributes to an innovative organization. We call this creative contention. In the next chapter we offer a process that can achieve this goal.

CHAPTER FIVE

CREATIVE CONTENTION

The most gifted members of the human species are at their creative best when they cannot have their way.

ERIC HOFFER

In Chapter Three we demonstrated that the interest-based negotiation process is not only successful in reaching settlements that the parties are committed to but that the solutions tend to be creative. Two or more people, even though they are in conflict, can, by following a collaborative process, develop a solution that is more creative than they could devise alone. It is also more creative than they could achieve through more traditional conflict resolution methods. That is pretty impressive stuff!

In Part One of this book (Chapters One, Two, and Three), the focus was on creative *dispute resolution*. Figure 5.1 represents

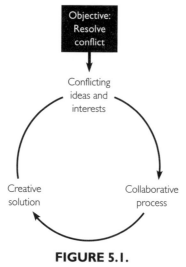

FIGURE 5.1.
Objective: Resolve Conflict

the use of the interest-based model. In this illustration the objective is to resolve the conflict between the parties. By exploring their conflicting interests and following a collaborative process, the parties can arrive at a creative solution.

Suppose we change the focus to creative *problem solving.* In concept we enter the system at a different point (see Figure 5.2).

The objective now is to generate creativity. By eliciting and exploring the diverse ideas and interests of the participants (who may not necessarily feel that they are in conflict) and

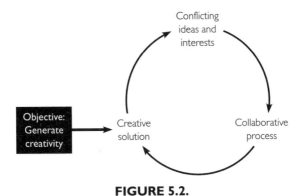

FIGURE 5.2.
Objective: Generate Creativity

using a similar collaborative process, they can arrive at the creative solution they were seeking.

As we explained in the previous chapter, conflict can play an important role in generating innovative responses to the complex problems organizations are facing today. The process of positive, productive conflict is what we term *creative contention.*

So how do we get the benefits of conflict without its costs? We start with a key canon for managing conflict: *be hard on the problem but soft on the people.* Some groups are too anxious to maintain harmony. They are soft on the people and soft on the problem. In other words people are so concerned about sparing one another's feelings that they do not say what they really believe about proposed ideas. They do not debate vigorously enough to contribute to creative solutions.

Other groups are too contentious. They are hard on the problem and hard on the people as well. Participants are single-minded in advancing their own ideas. They do not contribute to group creativity because they do not listen to or build on other people's ideas.

The goal of the creative contention process is to encourage people to tackle problems without tackling each other. By adapting the interest-based negotiation model, we can achieve this goal. In some ways it is easier to apply this model to working groups and teams than to apply it to disputing parties. Team members come together for the purpose of solving problems and usually do not bring the additional baggage of serious, unresolved disputes. Therefore the focus of the process can be on generating creativity and consensus rather than on resolving dysfunctional conflict. Even though we would not have to spend as much time up front resolving disputes, we would still need to manage the contention to keep it constructive and focused on creativity.

Creative contention depends on the interaction of four important components:

- A *process* that fosters the competition of ideas while encouraging the cooperation of people.

- Diverse *participants* who support the overall objectives of the group, are comfortable with conflict, and are good interest-based negotiators.

- A *leader* who understands and appreciates creative contention and has the mediation skills to manage the process.

- An *organizational culture* that is supportive of the process and the people.

We devote this chapter to an exploration of these components. The concepts are equally applicable to teams, departments, committees, or any other collection of people who must work together to achieve common goals.

THE CREATIVE CONTENTION PROCESS

In Chapter Two we presented our approach to collaborative conflict resolution in three stages:

Stage 1: Determine the underlying causes of the conflict. In particular, determine whether or not interpersonal issues are significant contributors to the conflict.

Stage 2: Deal with significant interpersonal issues first.

Stage 3: Then resolve the substantive issues.

In conflict resolution Stages 1 and 2 are critical because organizational conflict often has a significant relationship component. The interpersonal issues may provide the clue to resolving the conflict. Sometimes the entire conflict may, in fact, be interpersonal. In any event resolving the relationship issues will facilitate solving the substantive issues.

In creative contention the focus is on Stage 3. People are being brought together to solve problems creatively; presumably they are not in conflict with one another. Nevertheless it is wise to check on relationship issues both before and during problem solving, because interpersonal problems get in the way of creative contention. For creative contention to work, people must be prepared to express, challenge, and defend ideas vigorously and openly without attacking other people or being afraid of being attacked. If there are issues between participants that raise these concerns, they should be dealt with first.

Let us think again in terms of three stages (actions):

Stage 1: Identify interpersonal conflicts between participants.

Stage 2: Resolve significant interpersonal conflicts.

Stage 3: Work on creative problem solving.

Identify Interpersonal Conflicts Between Participants
The first stage is to determine whether or not interpersonal issues between participants might interfere with collaborative problem solving. In many cases the leader knows about rela-

tionship difficulties because of familiarity with the participants. When the leader does not know all of the members, interviews with participants or others might uncover interpersonal issues. For example, the leader might ask a participant: "Have you had any dealings with any other member of the group that might inhibit your ability to express yourself openly in group sessions?"

By carefully observing participants' behavior in introductory group meetings, the leader might discover other relationship problems that could then be explored in private interviews. The idea is to identify any pairs or small clusters of people who need to work out their interpersonal issues before participating in group problem-solving meetings. Otherwise, hidden agendas and gamesmanship will undermine collaboration.

It is important to continually monitor interpersonal relations within the group because the creative contention process might trigger or awaken relationship issues.

Resolve Significant Interpersonal Conflicts
Often there will be no serious relationship issues. In those cases the group can move on to Stage 3—creative problem solving. However, when interpersonal problems exist, the leader should deal with these in a way similar to that described in Chapter Two.

If any of the members resist taking part in addressing these interpersonal issues, the leader must decide whether or not to replace them on the team. This will depend on the leader's assessment of the importance and uniqueness of the members' potential contribution on the one hand and the possible disruption of creative contention on the other. Sometimes it is possible to structure the process to reduce the disruptive effect of interpersonal tensions.

Work on Creative Problem Solving
This stage is the essence of creative contention. In most cases the process begins here. Figure 5.3 illustrates the seven-step creative contention process, which we now explain in detail.

Some people might feel that it is contradictory to depend on such a structured process to generate creativity. However, we agree with a statement by the renowned expert on creativity, Edward de Bono (1986): "My preference is to treat creativity as a logical process rather than a matter of talent or mystique" (p. 114).

1. *Introduce the process and define the problem.* This is an important step, although it is often glossed over. This is the leader's opportunity to lay the groundwork for everything that follows by making clear the objectives of the exercise, the process to be followed, the ground rules, and so on. It is

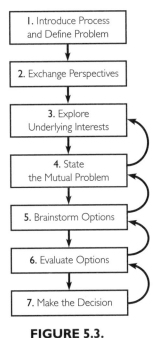

FIGURE 5.3.
The Creative Contention Process

important for the leader to set the right tone—one of *collaboration*. People should be welcomed and thanked for agreeing to participate. This is a good opportunity to model the collaborative process. The leader should take control of the discussion but should remain open to questions and suggestions for modifications. These are some of the important items to cover.

The Problem To Be Solved

At this point the leader should explain the objective. What problem has the group been asked to solve? Is that really the problem? Is the group permitted to negotiate modifications to the problem statement, or has it been fixed by more senior management? What time, process, and resource constraints have been placed on the group? Time should be taken to clarify these issues and get understanding and agreement. Too often people rush into solutions before they have properly understood the nature and scope of the problem.

Members of the group may have strong differences on the right solution, but everyone should make a commitment to work on the same problem. If some people are unable to accept the final definition of the problem or are unwilling to work on it, they should be asked to withdraw from the process.

Alternative to a Negotiated Solution

In conflict resolution (as we explained in Chapter Two) BATNA stands for "best alternative to a negotiated agreement" (Fisher and Ury, 1991). Each party in a dispute should understand his or her alternatives in the event that negotiations break down. This reality check often increases people's flexibility.

In creative contention, members of the group should be informed of what will happen should the group be unable to reach a decision. If this is expressed appropriately, it may motivate members to take the process seriously.

> *Sy:* I was facilitating a task force made up of (mainly male) middle-level managers who were commissioned to recommend a strategy to the CEO with respect to promoting women into senior management. The CEO was concerned that some of the men on the team might believe that it was in their interest to delay or obstruct the process. He attended the first meeting and, along with other introductory remarks, said this: "In three months I am going to announce a strategy for accomplishing this objective. You have an opportunity to stop me from taking an approach that you might not like by giving me a rational plan."

This statement was effective because, first, it made members aware that the alternative to their inability to make recommendations would *not* be delays or termination of the plan to promote women to senior positions. Second, by leaving unspoken what Plan B might be, the CEO raised the possibility that they might not like Plan B and so should pay attention to developing Plan A.

The Process
All participants should understand the process, including the steps and the time table. This allows them to participate in an intelligent way by letting them know when they will have the chance to put their proposals forward, raise questions and

objections, argue their points, and so on. If people do not know whether or when certain actions are provided for, they will raise issues too early in the process.

In addition to determining the structure of the process, the leader should set the tone. This includes an expectation of collaboration, a striving for consensus, a climate of friendly rivalry, and a relaxed attitude. The leader should also encourage participants not to take disagreements personally.

Ground Rules

The group should establish its own norms for the discussion. The purpose of the norms is to facilitate the contribution of all team members. The leader might ask, "What ground rules would be helpful in making sure that everyone's ideas get a full and fair hearing?" In response participants might decide that people should not interrupt each other and should speak respectfully and accept the principle that all ideas are worthy of a respectful hearing.

The issue of confidentiality should be discussed. All discussions of sensitive issues should be kept confidential unless everyone agrees to disclose specific items or disclose certain information to specific individuals. This invites people to be open in presenting and debating ideas. The leader may have to clarify with his or her superiors any exceptions to confidentiality and raise that with the group. It is essential that all participants and their managers understand the ground rule on confidentiality. Otherwise people may feel betrayed, and this will hurt morale, injure the leader's reputation, and reduce people's willingness to participate on future teams.

Decision-Making Rules

The team needs to consider how decisions will be made. Will it be by majority rule, by decision of the leader, or by consensus? Consensus is the most appropriate decision rule for creative contention because it maximizes the in-depth discussion of the issues. Consensus means that every member of the team accepts the decision and is willing to help implement it. It does not necessarily mean that everyone thinks it was the best decision. However, it does mean that all members feel that they have had a fair chance to have their views heard and considered and that they understand the rationale for the decision.

Gaining consensus can be frustrating at times, especially for those who like quick decisions. However, the fact that it slows down the decision-making process has definite benefits. That way all the important concerns can get raised and discussed. Gaining consensus empowers people and gives them a feeling of being part of the solution. Finally, it ensures that everyone is committed to implementing whatever decision gets made.

The group should agree on a back-up decision-making plan in case consensus proves impossible within the time constraints. This might include a unilateral decision by the team leader or a majority vote. By making this clear from the start of the process, there will be no surprises and objections when the time comes to make that call. And knowing the back-up approach might make people more flexible in accepting a consensus decision.

2. *Exchange perspectives.* At this point the team leader should invite members to explain their perspectives on the problem, including their experience with the subject, the constituents they represent, concerns they might have about the problem, and the broad interests they feel must be addressed.

Some people may have preferred solutions to the problem; others may not. The leader should ask that people defer offering proposals until later in the process.

3. *Explore underlying interests.* Once people's perspectives have been shared, discussion of interests can begin. The key question that people should be answering is, "What are the important interests (hopes, needs, concerns, values, priorities, and assumptions) that should be satisfied by any solution, and why are they important?" Those interests may be of three general types:

- *Organizational interests:* those that primarily meet the needs of the organization (such as providing better service to customers or reducing costs)

- *Constituent interests:* those that mainly meet the needs of the people represented by the speaker (such as making use of skills they have developed or saving their jobs)

- *Personal interests:* those that mainly meet the speaker's own interests (such as getting a promotion or a bonus or avoiding the prospect of relocating)

The team needs to know which kinds of interest are behind the proposal. Not because one kind is good and another kind is bad (having all these interests is normal) but because the first focus of the group should be on organizational interests. People's personal or constituent interests should be listened to and then *temporarily* put to the side. They should not shape the idea generation, the focus of which should be squarely on what is in the interests of the organization. However, if people are going to be prepared to commit to this larger goal, they will need to be assured that their other, more personal interests will be addressed fairly later in the process.

Barbara: While I was leading a group that was designing an important interagency conference, it became apparent that a pending strike might mean that one agency would not be able to participate. The representative of that agency was very committed to the project and had invested a lot of effort in the preparation. She proposed that the entire conference be postponed and was hurt when I suggested that we look at options, including continuing with the conference. I acknowledged the wonderful contribution she had made and reassured her that we would consider her personal concerns but suggested that we first explore what would be in everyone's interests.

In the end the various agencies decided that the unique feature of the conference was the modeling of cooperation between all of the agencies. Solidarity was important, and therefore the consensus reached was to postpone the conference. In this way the result satisfied the organizational interests. A secondary benefit was that the individual representative's personal interests were also met.

Dealing with personal or constituent interests is tricky; personal interests are especially so. Unless there is a high degree of trust among the participants, people will be reluctant to share some of their objectives or concerns. They will also be skeptical about the willingness of others to address their personal needs. Therefore they often become a hidden agenda that disrupts the process.

Let us take an example to illustrate the seven-step process. To demonstrate the application of creative contention we will modify the residential care example described in Chapter Two. Suppose there had been *no interpersonal conflict* between the director of nursing and the residential director. Imagine that the executive director has brought them together to recommend to the board a model for providing medical care for the residents.

As the first step of the creative contention process the executive director poses this question: "What approach should we use in providing medical care to our residents?" The executive director explains that the board is expecting a recommendation from the three of them and that this is their opportunity to propose a workable model that meets the needs of the residents and that they and their staffs can live with. They spend some time discussing ground rules and who will make the recommendation if they cannot reach consensus.

When asked to explain their perspectives (the second step), the nursing director advocates a centralized model in which decisions about health care would be made by the specially trained nurses and doctors at the head office, who would also treat the residents. People needing treatment would be brought to the central facility unless they were too ill, in which case health care staff members would treat them at their group residence.

The residential director favors a community-based model. She proposes that the residential coordinator at each home would make decisions about when and where to seek treatment for residents, and most of the treatment would be provided by local doctors.

In the third step the nursing director explains the interests underlying her plan:

- Residents would receive the best-quality care because the internal nurses and doctors are specially trained in the kinds of potentially life-threatening medical conditions frequently faced by the residents.
- There would be a continuity of care because the records and providers would be in-house.
- Further, on a personal level she (the nursing director) would be able to fulfill her professional liability for the health of the residents.
- On a constituent level the nurses and in-house doctors are concerned that some of them may lose their jobs if local providers are used.

The residential director provides her rationale:

- Treatment would be provided in a way that is convenient for both the residents and the staff.
- Most of the ailments are identical to those faced by others in the community: colds, flu, minor injuries, and so on and require no specialized care.
- The proposal is consistent with the organization's stated objective of providing a homelike environment for the residents.
- On a constituent level the residential coordinators believe that they should act in place of parents, making all parental decisions for their charges.

At this point the executive director leads a discussion of the rationales, encouraging respectful questions and explanations. There might be some discussion of the types of illnesses and their implications, the skills of local doctors, the expectation of residents' families, and so on. There would probably be some clarification of the executive director's expectations about the ultimate responsibility for patient welfare, by way of addressing the personal and constituent concerns on both sides.

4. *Articulate the mutual problem statement.* At the start of the process the leader stated the problem that the group would be expected to solve. Now after exploring the important interests, the leader is in a position to expand the problem statement into what we call the mutual problem statement. This is probably best explained by continuing the residential care example given earlier.

> The initial problem presented by the executive director was, "What approach should we use in providing medical care to our residents?" Now that all of the interests have been explored—setting aside for the moment the personal and constituent interests—the executive director can expand the problem statement:
>
> Our mutual challenge is to find a way of providing high-quality medical care to our residents that
>
> - Is appropriate for the kinds of medical conditions (both routine and life-threatening) faced by the residents
> - Is convenient for both the residents and the staff
> - Allows for complete and accurate record keeping

- Is consistent with the organization's stated objective of providing a homelike environment for the residents

The leader should invite the group to comment on and suggest modifications to the proposed mutual problem statement before finalizing it.

5. *Brainstorm options.* Now the real creativity begins. The goal of brainstorming is to set free the imagination by a process of suspended judgment. The brainstorming process was invented by Alex Osborn in 1938 for his advertising firm. He believed that of all the requirements for imaginative thinking, "the most important is to guard against being both critical and creative at one and the same time" (1963, p. 149).

With the benefit of having listened to the ideas and concerns of others, and with the articulation of the mutual problem statement, the brainstorming session ought to produce more creative options.

The leader should explain the rules of brainstorming:

- There will be no discussion of the ideas until after the brainstorming process.
- The more options the better.
- All ideas are welcome.

- Combinations of options are sought.

- Proposing or hearing an option does not mean accepting it.

Brainstorming highlights the real value of diversity. The more disparate the perspectives, the more different options will surface, thus opening up the prospect of creative solutions.

However, brainstorming may be hindered because people are afraid to propose unpopular or unusual options. This may be out of a sense of loyalty to other members, or a fear of ridicule, or a reluctance to oppose members who are more powerful. If the leader is concerned about this, he or she should arrange for ideas to be gathered in less threatening ways, such as by sending ideas anonymously to someone who will transcribe them or by using small groups to propose options.

> *Sy:* We once worked with a group of technical specialists who were wrestling with some organizational issues. The trust level within the group was quite low. The company had a "Decision Support Centre" that consisted of a boardroom table with a computer terminal at each chair. Each participant entered his suggestion on his terminal. The system then stripped away any identifiers and randomly transferred the idea to someone else's terminal. That person was invited to modify or critique the idea

(again anonymously) and send it on. This approach resulted in lots of options and some very honest and useful comments. And the "tekkies" loved the process.

6. *Evaluate options.* Now that all the ideas are out on the table, the vigorous debate and evaluation of the ideas can commence. The flaws of some ideas will be exposed, the potential of others realized.

Participants should still use respectful communication in asking questions, answering them, and expressing reservations. Ideas should be explored fully, and efforts should be made to improve problematic ones before they are rejected.

Incomplete options can be combined or new options put forth. Rarely do you get a complete solution from any one option. It is important to take the step of bundling or packaging options before options can be properly evaluated. This process can produce a number of unexpected and creative alternatives.

Once options are bundled, the two or three that have the most support or that reflect the strongest division of opinion should go through one additional step. All members of the team should be invited to comment on the benefits of and the negative consequences of each option, and these ideas should be displayed for all to see.

There are several advantages to this approach. First, the most significant options get a full and respectful analysis. Second, proponents of an option are asked to look at their own proposals critically, and the option's "opponents" are asked to comment on what they think is beneficial about it. This builds bridges of understanding between individuals with different viewpoints. Third, the process often pries people free from positional thinking and stimulates the creation of new options that had not been considered or would not have been received favorably if they had been put forth by an opponent. Finally, people find it easier to let go of an idea that others won't endorse if they feel that the idea has been given a respectful hearing.

Often the roadblock to this exploration is the anxiety expressed by some team members about examining unpopular or unconventional solutions. Frequently there is a chorus of, "We shouldn't even be discussing that option because it is disloyal to. . . . " or "That option has never been done in this organization" or some other emotional response. It is helpful to remind participants that discussing an idea doesn't mean it will be accepted, just that it will be considered.

A good way to evaluate and choose among ideas is to establish some objective criteria. Objective criteria protect decision making from becoming a contest between personal preferences. Those criteria might include the following:

- How well do the options satisfy the mutual problem statement?

- How costly are the options?

- How easily and quickly can the options be implemented?

- Are options legal and in line with company policy?

- How well do options satisfy personal and constituent interests?

At this point these personal and constituent interests can be discussed, and some real negotiating can happen. Someone might say, "In order for my people to buy into that idea, they will need assurances regarding staffing and other support to do the job." If someone's personal concerns are too sensitive to raise with the group, the team leader may provide an opportunity to speak privately with the person at some break in the process. The more the team develops relationships of trust among its members, the more willing people will be to discuss their personal concerns openly.

Some participants may be reluctant to raise personal interests even in private. Or there may be some hidden agendas. It may not be possible to identify all of these kinds of issues, but the leader should look for situations in which someone refuses to accept an option that appears to meet all of that person's stated interests. This could then form the basis of a private discussion.

7. *Make the decision and plan its implementation.* It is time for the team to make a decision. The leader can try to ascertain where people stand and what would be needed to reach consensus. If the group remains divided, the leader can either continue to work toward consensus in an interest-based way or adopt the back-up decision-making process that everyone has agreed on.

The more important the decision and the more necessary the commitment of the participants to implement the decision, the better it is to try for consensus. However, if a decision is urgently needed, the leader will have to move more quickly to the back-up decision-making process.

However the decision is reached, it should be spelled out clearly, specifying the people responsible for actions and the target dates. Unless this is done, conflict will arise based on different recollections and interpretations of the agreement.

PARTICIPANTS, LEADERS, AND CULTURE

Earlier in this chapter we identified four components to effective creative contention. We have already discussed the process and now want to add the three other components:

- Diverse *participants* who support the overall objectives of the group, are comfortable with conflict, and are good interest-based negotiators

- A *leader* who understands and appreciates creative contention and has the mediation skills to manage the process

- An *organizational culture* that is supportive of the process and the people.

The Participants

Members of problem-solving groups are usually selected because of their knowledge of the subjects being discussed. An ideal team should cover the entire range of expertise needed to understand and analyze the issues under discussion. In assembling a team to design a strategy for entering a new geographic market, for example, management would probably appoint experts in the major product lines, people familiar with the new market, possibly a human resources professional, someone from the financial area, an information technology specialist, and so on. The team would also be likely to include someone who is familiar with scheduling the tasks, preparing budgets, and monitoring progress (some members might cover several of these tasks). Such a group would have a degree of diversity based on their content knowledge.

A group made up of people selected only for their content knowledge might or might not have other differences. We have already argued that groups have more creative potential if they are diverse, so we would suggest trying to build in diversity based on gender, culture, age, and profession. It may be helpful in some situations to include outsiders to the organization.

A diverse group has the potential to be very creative, but it might just as easily turn out to be pedantic and unimaginative or contentious and uncooperative. The following are some additional attributes that leaders might look for in order to promote creative contention:

- *Participants should share the important objectives of the team,* even though they may have very different perspectives and ideas on the best ways to achieve the objectives. A team composed of people who disagree significantly about the objectives of the team will soon be embroiled in dysfunctional conflict.

- *Participants should be confident in their own ability to succeed in new situations.* One reason that people might resist others' ideas is a concern that they will suffer personally if those ideas are accepted. For example, they might be afraid that they do not possess the skills needed to cope with a particular solution. However, if participants believe they can adapt to change, they will be less likely to oppose ideas their teammates put forward.

- *Participants should be reasonably representative of and respected by their constituents.* This ensures that they can present the interests of the constituents to the team and that they can help sell the team's decisions to their constituents.

Remember that this is one of the strengths of diversity. People who lack confidence in their ability to do this will be reluctant to accept creative ideas.

- *Participants should be able to view issues broadly and with a future perspective.* During brainstorming sessions participants must be able to let go of the present constraints and allow their imagination some free rein. People who are too detail oriented and analytical often find it hard to be creative or to accept creative leaps by others.

- *Participants should be welcoming of differences and open to new ideas.* Creative contention requires that people see the value in diversity. They must be prepared to suspend their critical faculties until all ideas are on the table and to evaluate ideas based on their merits rather than on the identity of the person putting the idea forward.

- *Participants should be good interest-based negotiators.* They must be willing and able to advocate for their ideas and interests even when they know that others disagree. They must also have good listening skills so that they can hear and understand the essence of other people's ideas. The creative contention process is a negotiation process.

It is not necessary for individuals to be particularly creative in their own right. If they are able to apply the skills and attitudes listed, the process will generate creativity. Of course, individual creativity can be helpful, but even a whole team of creative individuals may not be able to generate and implement creative ideas if the other attributes are not present. It is easy but painful to imagine a room full of inventive geniuses, all putting forward novel concepts without listening to the ideas of others and therefore unable to integrate the individual concepts and unwilling to help implement anything other than their own proposals.

Members of a diverse team have many areas of potential contention with one another:

- They may have different educational and professional backgrounds.
- They may have had different experiences and may view things through different lenses.
- They may interpret information differently.
- They may represent different constituencies.
- They may be bound by different professional codes of ethics.
- They may come from different cultures and thus may have different values and beliefs.

This potential contention is not a bad thing; in fact, these differences are the very reasons for deciding to use such teams. The challenge is to encourage people to put these important differences on the table, argue their merits vigorously, and at the end of the day develop creative, high-quality solutions that all members can buy into and sell to others.

The Leader

The second critical component of creative contention is a leader who has the attitude and ability to take the participants through the process. We are using the term *leader* as a catch-all to include anyone who directs a group of people to accomplish common objectives. Leaders might be managers or executives at any organizational level, task force or project managers, or committee chairs.

Leaders need management skills and some content knowledge. They should also have the same skills and attitudes described earlier for participants in creative contention. In addition the leader should have the following attributes:

- *The leader should understand and believe in the creative contention process.* He or she should be confident in the usefulness of interest-based processes to generate creative solutions.

- *The leader should adopt a participatory, consensus-building style of leadership.* An authoritarian or hierarchical leadership style will likely short-circuit the exploration or stifle the participation necessary for creative outcomes.

- *The leader should be comfortable with conflict.* Many of us are very uncomfortable in situations involving conflict, so we try to avoid contentious situations or minimize conflict when it arises. We also tend to resent those who raise contentious issues. But creative contention is a process that actually requires that people raise and debate their differences. Therefore the leader must be comfortable with contention, see its value, and, dare we say, welcome the challenge!

Human Research Management Research Quarterly (Allen and Hecht, 2000) reports that surveys from 223 employees representing twenty-four teams in four large companies showed that "conflict management was correlated to both perceptions of team effectiveness and team satisfaction. This means that team members who were able to resolve their conflicts perceived themselves to be more effective and were more satisfied" and vice versa (p. 3).

- *The leader should have the mediation skills needed to facilitate the process.* Mediation is a form of facilitation used in brokering agreements between people who are in conflict. In an ideal world team members would be such skilled negotiators that they would not need mediation, but it would be very rare for everyone on a team to be equally good negotiators. And sometimes even excellent negotiators need a helping hand. The idea that a leader should be a good conflict resolver is not a new concept, although it is slow in taking hold. Dean Tjosvold, who writes about the value of conflict in organizations, says, "Rather than be a judge and arbitrator, a leader is a mediator who assists" (1995, p. 186).

Mediation skills include excellent communication skills, which are needed in order to help others listen and express themselves. Other skills include the ability to build trust, to anticipate and unblock impasses, and to balance the power differences among team members, thus ensuring that the team as a whole achieves the best possible results. In addition, a mediator must have the patience to fully explore the needs and perspectives of all participants without rushing to a solution.

A leader may employ a trained (internal or external) facilitator to guide certain important problem-solving meetings, but if creative contention is to become part of the culture of the organization, leaders must develop their own mediation skills.

- *The leader should be able to model the behaviors expected of the participants.* These include speaking and listening respectfully, not interrupting, putting organizational interests first, separating ideas from identity, and so on. It is all well and good to set out expected norms at the beginning of the process, but people tend to believe those rules if the leader follows them.

Some people come by these attributes naturally, but most of us have to learn at least some of them. And the good news is that they can be learned. Many organizations are now providing training in conflict resolution, interest-based negotiation, communication skills, and mediation for team leaders and others in management positions.

A leader using a creative contention process may have to *instigate* conflict, not just resolve it. If the group seems to be too quick in reaching consensus or too dismissive of outside concerns, the leader should raise the issues and try to generate some controversy. Like a chemist trying to get just the right chemical reaction, the leader of the team must decide whether it is time to heat up the mixture or cool it down because it is overheating.

The Organizational Culture

The final component necessary for successful creative contention is a supportive organizational culture. You cannot just insert a process that values creativity, diversity, and conflict into an organization that is not receptive to them. A supportive organization culture includes the following attributes:

- *Creativity is valued.* Creative contention will work best in an organization that is always looking for inventive ways to deal with continual changes in its external environment.

- *Risk taking is encouraged.* People are encouraged to take intelligent risks, and mistakes are viewed as learning opportunities.

- *Diversity is welcomed.* The organization has a workforce that is diverse in many ways, and it values that diversity.

- *Decision making is shared.* People are expected to participate in making decisions in their areas of expertise.

- *The wisdom of groups is respected.* It makes regular use of diverse teams to solve problems or deal with complex day-to-day issues because of a general belief in the creative potential of such groups

- *Conflict is normalized.* Members of the organization accept the inevitability of conflict, understand the importance of managing that conflict, and are confident in their conflict management skills. People are not afraid to disagree with one another, but they do it respectfully. They do not personalize disagreements. They understand that collaborative negotiation leads to better, more acceptable and more creative decisions.

An organization that demonstrates these qualities tends to attract and retain the kind of people who can lead and participate in creative contention. It also gives people the assurance that they are participating in a process that is consistent with the values of the organization and that their work will be taken seriously.

Organizations vary in their possession of these attributes, but that should not be an excuse for avoiding creative contention.

Instead they should strive to enhance their receptivity in order to take advantage of the potential benefits. Richard Tanner Pascale (1990) describes how Ford Motor Company in the 1980s succeeded in turning a culture that bred dysfunctional conflict into one that fostered positive conflict. It did so by training people in conflict management and by reconfiguring its compensation policies to reward collaborative behavior. In fact, the company's first step was to encourage contention about its own negative practices. For many organizations that may be the best first step toward cultural change.

BENEFITS OF CREATIVE CONTENTION

Creative contention has several important benefits over other group problem-solving processes:

- Group problem-solving processes usually seem to assume that participants come to the table ready to work together constructively. The creative contention process acknowledges that interpersonal conflicts may exist between group members and that these issues could interfere with collaborative problem solving. It addresses these potentially disruptive conflicts up front.

- Many group processes tend to avoid conflict in an effort to maintain group harmony. They use diversity to generate a variety of ideas. They are inclusive, in that they try to construct solutions that include everyone's ideas. Inclusion is good, but sidestepping areas of disagreement is not. Creative contention also tries to include as many ideas as possible through the mutual problem statement and the combining and evaluation of options. However, it recognizes that some ideas and interests may actually conflict and some may be mutually exclusive. It uses interest-based negotiation as a mechanism for resolving these conflicts.

- Problem-solving processes often overlook or gloss over personal and constituent interests, and these processes assume that all participants will be able to focus exclusively on the common organizational objectives. Although creative contention acknowledges the primacy of organizational objectives, it recognizes the important part played by the personal concerns and needs of the participants and their constituents in gaining their support for the decisions reached in the group.

In summary, creative contention is more realistic than many other approaches, in that it recognizes and makes use of natural conflict that exists in organizations. However, nothing is perfect. In the next chapter we anticipate some concerns or problems that could occur with the creative contention process.

CHAPTER SIX

PLAYING WITH FIRE?

○

We remain in the Dark Ages in grasping the value of contention . . . and how it can be constructively harnessed.

RICHARD TANNER PASCALE

In our experience conflict often provides the combustible spark that ignites creativity. If the spark is too weak, creativity fails to ignite. If the conflict is poorly managed, the flames may burn out of control, consuming the energy of the parties and sapping their capacity for problem solving. If it is well managed, contention heightens the parties' concentration on problem solving, thus increasing the likelihood of an innovative outcome.

Two significant risks are inherent in creative contention: (1) there will be too much contention, or (2) there will not be enough. Of these two possibilities the first is the most worrisome to most people. Because most of us are not comfortable with conflict, the thought of a process being initiated for creative problem solving and then degenerating into dysfunctional conflict is enough to discourage us from even trying it.

In her book *The Argument Culture: Moving from Debate to Dialogue,* Deborah Tannen recognizes the creative potential of conflict but cautions against seeing opposition as an end itself. In her view our adversarial culture has serious limitations: "Our determination to pursue truth by setting up a fight between two sides leads us to believe that every issue has two sides—no more, no less. If both sides are given a forum to confront each other, all the relevant information will emerge, and the best case will be made for each side. But opposition does not lead to truth when an issue is not composed of two opposing sides but is a crystal of many sides. Often the truth is in the complex middle, not the oversimplified extremes" (1999, p. 10).

The second possibility—not enough contention—does not scare people as much, but it has the potential to undermine the whole concept.

In this chapter we look at the risks of too much and not enough contention and some of the things that we can do to reduce those risks.

RISK 1: TOO MUCH CONFLICT

Earlier in the book we referred to a Canadian Royal Commission that ended up in recriminations and dysfunctional conflict. This is the kind of nightmare that haunts leaders of project teams, multidisciplinary teams, and committees; it is not uncommon.

The risks are obvious. You have a complex and sensitive issue that requires a creative solution. You set up a task force to address the issue, and you appoint a leader who is committed to developing an innovative response. You select members who have different perspectives based on their diverse backgrounds and constituencies. You hope (and have reason to think) that the members care about the issue and have given it considerable thought before they were appointed to the task force. And then things fall apart in one or more of the following ways:

- Participants have already taken rigid positions and are not prepared to consider other options.

- Participants have preconceived biases about the motivation or credibility of other members and thus discount their ideas.

- Participants' ideas are devalued because of who offered them, not because of the merits of the ideas.

- People with similar outlooks start to band together in cliques that are unreceptive to the ideas of "outsiders."

- Participants express themselves in aggressive and disrespectful ways that alienate others.

- Members refuse to consider other options because they are afraid that their constituents will equate flexibility with disloyalty.

- Participants report to outsiders on the internal proceedings of the group. This violates the expectation of confidentiality of other members and makes them reluctant to share information in the discussions.

- People ridicule other people's options, leading to counterattacks by some members and nonparticipation by others.

- At the end of the process consensus is unattainable, and dissenters issue one or more minority reports.

Although you were trying to foster the competition of ideas and the cooperation of people, what you got was the competition of both. No wonder that some people shy away from potentially high-conflict situations. However, in our opinion such avoidance of contention would be ill advised because the potential benefits are worth the risks.

Other writers have stated similar views. Dean Tjosvold, in his book *The Conflict-Positive Organization* (1992), suggests that advocacy teams be used to stir up contention. Members of a team are assigned alternative positions to defend. They each present their arguments and then strive to integrate their different ideas. Tjosvold feels that conflict can build trust and creativity, whereas the avoidance of conflict or the poor management of it will have opposite effect on a team.

In an article titled "How Management Teams Can Have A Good Fight," Kathleen M. Eisenhardt, Jean L. Kahwajy, and L. J. Bourgeois III (1997) report on their ten-year study of decision making in top-management teams. They found that teams that managed conflict well arrived at better decisions in less time than the teams that handled conflict poorly, and the cohesion of the group was strengthened. How did the successful teams manage the conflict? Eisenhardt and her colleagues found that successful groups used these techniques:

- They used facts and information rather than opinions to make their case.

- They allowed many options to be on the table, thereby making choices less black-and-white and allowing people to shift positions without losing face.

- Team members emphasized common goals and collaboration.

- Team members injected humor into the decision-making process. A positive mood, according to research, allows more forgiveness and creativity.

149

- The groups had a fair process for decision making. Fair processes can lead people to accept decisions with which they disagree. Fair processes require balanced power structures, somewhere between the extremes of autocratic rule and weak leadership. In other words you need strong leaders balanced by strong members.

- Successful teams tried to achieve consensus but did not force it. Their backup was that the top manager would make a decision (with input) if consensus proved impossible. Forcing consensus led to bitter conflict because everyone had veto power over a decision.

These prescriptions are comparable to the findings of Tjosvold in his own research. And our experience is similar. Each of the four components of creative contention (process, participants, leader, and organizational culture) that we described in Chapter Five plays an important role in keeping conflict creative. Without going into great detail and duplicating the information in Chapter Five, we will highlight some of the key actions that can minimize destructive conflict.

ORGANIZATIONAL CULTURE ISSUES

Here are a few suggestions for addressing cultural issues:

1. Build a culture that encourages collaboration rather than competition. Introduce a compensation system that rewards

team performance. This is not done in many organizations, and it presents an impediment to cooperation. For example, if my compensation is based on performance in my home department, I may be reluctant to consider options that are not in the best interests of my department, even though they are best for the corporation.

2. Hire and promote people who are collaborative and team oriented, who have good communication and interpersonal skills, and who are comfortable with contention.

3. Clarify and emphasize corporate goals over and above the goals of departments or other constituencies. This will increase flexibility in considering options that best meet the needs of the entire organization. In many organizations subunits evolve their own cultures that become disconnected from the corporate culture over time. Unless these are reviewed and adjusted regularly, team members from separate areas may have seriously conflicting values and goals.

4. Offer training programs in communication, conflict management, negotiation, mediation, and facilitation. Encourage people at various levels to take the appropriate training.

5. Help people adapt to change. People who believe that they will be given the necessary retraining and support to allow them to succeed in the changed environment will be more

willing to consider creative options and to accept innovative solutions.

LEADERSHIP ISSUES

The leader's attitudes and actions can reduce destructive conflict. The following are some helpful suggestions:

1. Appoint a leader who understands and trusts the process. Otherwise he or she will be tempted to abandon it when the going gets tough. The process is *about* conflict; there is supposed to be contention. It is important not to back off when it occurs.

2. The leader should appreciate the importance of relationship issues and should be sensitive to subtle signs of tension. This may be a problem in technical groups: members are often reluctant to share interpersonal concerns, and leaders are not sufficiently tuned in to nonverbal cues.

3. The leader should take an evenhanded approach. People have to believe that their ideas and arguments have the potential to influence the decision or they will find other, less constructive ways to exert influence or block a decision.

4. The leader should be aware that sometimes the best work gets done outside the meeting. The Japanese have a practice

known as *nemawashi,* where managers talk privately with
each participant prior to a meeting to get everyone's opinions
and coordinate interests. The practice is based on the assumption that people are more likely to present a "false front" in
public and more likely to be honest in private (Tannen, 1994,
p. 305). The practice of holding private meetings is useful for
managing groups with different personality types. For example, in a group made up of introverts and extroverts, the
extroverts often monopolize meetings, usually unwittingly.
Introverts often have well-thought-out ideas, but these may
be lost to the team. Some private meetings with the introverts
can ensure that the group benefits from their valuable input.

5. Acknowledge individuals for their contribution to the team,
including a broad range of positive behaviors that help the
team function well and complete its task.

PARTICIPANT ISSUES

The following ideas should be considered when appointing
members to the team:

1. Select participants who accept the objectives of the team
and the benefits of collaboration.

2. Choose participants who are respected by the constituents
they represent and not excessively controlled by them. They

have to be confident that they can speak on behalf of their clientele and will be able to influence them to accept the decision of the group. Otherwise the participants will be unwilling to consider other options.

PROCESS ISSUES

The following suggestions about the process will minimize destructive conflict:

1. Identify and address preexisting interpersonal conflicts before attempting to address the substantive objectives of the group. Otherwise the process will be undermined by disrespect, formation of cliques, and rigidity that will not make sense in an objective context.

2. Make sure that everybody understands and accepts the idea of collaboration in general and the creative contention process in particular. Take time to explain and to answer questions.

3. Help the group define a complete set of ground rules. It is easier to get agreement on acceptable behavior before anybody has behaved unacceptably.

4. Post the objectives, the outline of the process, and the ground rules at every meeting.

5. Make sure that everybody understands the backup decision-making process in the event that consensus is impossible.

6. Step in early to head off disrespectful behavior (or other violations of the ground rules) so that it does not lead to retaliation or become the norm. Speak to difficult people in a private caucus so as not to embarrass them and entrench their behavior.

7. Ensure that unconventional ideas are given consideration just like other ideas. Do not take them off the table too quickly.

8. Explain the rules of brainstorming again, just before beginning that activity. Encourage lots of ideas and discourage comments, either positive or negative.

9. Separate "the singer from the song." Discourage the practice of identifying ideas with particular authors. If ideas are too attached to particular individuals, ego and politics may play a big role in the acceptance or rejection of those ideas. If necessary design a process to allow ideas to be submitted anonymously. Brainwriting (a process in which participants put their ideas in writing anonymously before circulating them) or electronic brainstorming processes have been used very effectively for this purpose (Mongeau and Morr, 1999).

10. Develop objective criteria for evaluating options to minimize the weight of subjective and interpersonal factors.

11. Pay attention to the personal and constituent interests. Very often these concerns undermine cooperation. Tell people up front that their concerns will be taken seriously. Use private caucuses and the promise of confidentiality to encourage people to raise these issues.

12. Allow participants time and opportunity to check back with their constituents at various points during the process as long as confidentiality is not violated. This reassures people that they will still be able to sell the decisions.

13. Give the group enough time to reach consensus, thus minimizing the perceived need for minority reports. Even if the leader must eventually make a unilateral decision, he or she should explain it carefully, acknowledging the concerns raised by the dissenters.

Following these suggestions should reduce the risk of too much conflict. Of course there are no guarantees. Even the most promising process can go wrong. If destructive conflict does become a serious problem, the process described in Chapter Two of this book will be helpful.

RISK 2: NOT ENOUGH CONFLICT

The effects of too little conflict are not as dangerous as those of too much. In fact, many people would feel more comfortable and view the process more positively if there's little conflict. They would probably use words like *harmonious* and *amicable* to describe the workings of the group. On the face of it consensus would be reached more easily. So what's the problem? In fact, several problems result from insufficient contention; some are potentially serious.

- *The solutions will be less creative than they could be.* If you accept the need for creativity and the link between creativity and conflict as set out in Chapter Four, then it is clear that too little conflict will result in a loss of creativity.

- *Consensus will be artificial.* The decisions reached may prove unworkable in practical or political terms because no one raised objections despite their misgivings.

- *The decision will be difficult to implement.* This follows from the previous point. If the decision does not really meet people's needs (because they did not sufficiently express and explain them), the participants will have little interest in making it work.

If you initiate a process that is contingent on the competition of ideas, be very careful to ensure that the competition really takes place. How do you do this? Here are some suggestions:

1. Encourage creative contention by reducing the possibility of destructive conflict. One reason people do not advocate strongly is fear that the situation might degenerate. If they can be reassured that this will not happen, they will be more forthcoming.

2. Emphasize that the task is important and that the group's decision will carry weight. Most people may not be willing to take risks for unimportant causes or when they believe that their input will not matter.

3. Encourage participants to think carefully about their BAT-NAs. What will happen if they do not put forward their ideas? What if there is an apparent consensus that does not take their issues into account?

4. Make the process informal. It is true that the creative contention process we described has a prescribed series of steps, but experienced leaders or facilitators learn how to reduce the formality without missing the essential components. Furthermore, even within the prescribed structure, the discussion and debate can be freewheeling.

5. Make the process fun. Show that it is acceptable to laugh, as long as it is not at other people's expense and does not derail the process. Use friendly rivalry and other methods to keep the energy level high.

6. Give people time to think about the issues before they have to put forward their ideas. This is particularly important for introverts. It might help to allow thinking time between certain steps in the process, such as before brainstorming.

7. Do not be afraid of silence. People are uncomfortable with silence; eventually someone will fill it, maybe with a creative idea.

8. Provide safe methods for raising difficult issues. Emphasize the confidentiality of the process. If necessary collect ideas, concerns, and comments anonymously (as described in Chapter Five).

9. Propose far-out options. Leaders or facilitators should refrain from putting their own ideas forward or proposing options because others may assume that the decision has already been made. However, if nobody else is actively engaging in creative thinking, the leader might get things rolling by making suggestions that are obviously pump-primers. "What if?" questions are often helpful. For example: "What if funding were not an issue, what possibilities would you consider?"

10. Find a devil's advocate. If participants appear reluctant to challenge ideas, encourage someone to raise questions just to set the tone. The leader might pose a hypothetical challenge

such as, "If someone were really looking for potential weaknesses in this idea, what could he say?"

11. Allow people to reflect for a day or more before a final decision is made. This may assure them that they will not be railroaded, and it may also lead to new insights and ideas.

The first time people participate in creative contention is the most difficult. They are being asked to take part in a process involving interpersonal risk, based on contention (which makes many of us uncomfortable), in pursuit of creativity—a nebulous concept. They may also be skeptical about management's seriousness in accepting the group's solutions. Once they have been through a successful process, however, they see that the risks are not as great as they thought, contention can be invigorating, and the solutions are indeed creative and accepted. Then they are hooked.

CHAPTER SEVEN

FROM CONFLICT
TO CREATIVITY

There are two kinds of truth, small truth and great truth. You
can recognize a small truth because its opposite is a falsehood.
The opposite of a great truth is another truth.

NIELS BOHR

For every one thousand books about the *costs* of conflict,
there may be one that talks about the *value* of conflict. In this
book we have addressed both topics, and we have tried to
distinguish between conflict that is unhealthy and conflict that
is beneficial. We are certainly not the first to speak of the creative potential of contention. Other authors have laid the
groundwork by demonstrating how some corporate cultures
suppress or avoid conflict to their detriment, whereas others
benefit from surfacing conflict and managing it effectively.
This book goes further than others in describing a specific
process for managing both the creative and destructive effects
of contention.

We have also integrated the resolution of interpersonal issues into the conflict management process. This expands on the first principle of interest-based negotiation: *separate the people from the problem.* Many dispute management writers and practitioners interpret this to mean: *ignore or paper over interpersonal issues and get on with addressing the real (substantive) conflicts.* This may work in disputes among people who will never have to deal with one another again, but in organizational conflict it is a sure recipe for continuing conflict.

This book may also be the first to explicitly suggest the application of the interest-based negotiation process for the purpose of generating creativity. The interest-based process has been used for years to resolve or prevent disputes. It has succeeded through its ability to open the minds of disputants, to transcend polarized positions, and to find creative alternatives. That ability led us to the possibilities of adapting such a process so that its raison d'être is innovation rather than conflict resolution.

We need creativity to resolve interpersonal conflict. We need conflict—the contention of ideas—to generate creativity. It is no good avoiding or suppressing conflict for the sake of harmony; but neither is it wise to encourage people to give a free rein to their emotions and just go at it. It is too easy for the competition of ideas to turn into the competition of people.

A collaborative process and a set of conflict management skills can ensure that positive conflict does not become personalized.

Perhaps it is the common view that creativity springs out of the minds of geniuses that has kept people from looking more closely at contention. We believe that organizations are now ready to recognize that creativity is largely a product of human interaction. In particular it is the interaction of people with different experiences and different ways of thinking that produces innovation. Organizations are increasingly ready to embrace a diverse workforce. Those shifts from autonomy to teamwork and from homogeneity to diversity indicate that we are on the brink of something interesting. Because we are bringing different people together to cooperate, we can expect more conflict. We can also anticipate some very innovative outcomes.

Too often words like *teamwork* and *consensus* have been misused as a way to stifle divergent viewpoints. An employee who argues strongly for his or her opinion may be accused of not being a team player. That culture will inhibit creative thought. Contention needs to be seen as necessary—as fun. Workplaces would be dull indeed if they had no conflict. Dysfunctional conflict, however, can drain the life force right out of people. We hope people will begin to look on dysfunctional conflict as a lost opportunity for creative communication. We hope they develop the skills and the courage to confront conflict in search of a better solution.

Above all we hope that some readers strongly disagree with what we have said. Contention is what makes life interesting.

References

Allen, N., and Hecht, T. D. "Team-Organization Alignment and Team Behaviour: Implications for Human Resource Management." *Human Resource Management Research Quarterly,* 2000, 4(3), 1–5.

Bohr, N. Quoted in W. Bennis, *On Becoming a Leader.* Menlo Park: Addison-Wesley, 1989.

Briggs, M. *Myers-Briggs Type Indicator.* Palo Alto, Calif.: Consulting Psychology Press, 1991.

Bush, R.A.B., and Folger, J. P. *The Promise of Mediation.* San Francisco: Jossey-Bass, 1994.

"Clayoquot Sound." Canadian Broadcasting Corporation, Aug. 24, 2000. Radio.

Cox, T., Jr. *Cultural Diversity in Organizations.* San Francisco: Berrett-Koehler, 1993.

de Bono, E. *Conflicts: A Better Way to Resolve Them.* New York: Penguin Books, 1986.

de Bono, E. *Six Thinking Hats.* London: Penguin Books, 1990.

Dimnet, E. Quoted in A.F. Osborn, *Applied Imagination: Principles and Procedures of Creative Problem Solving.* New York: Scribner, 1963.

Eisenhardt, K. M., Kahwajy, J. L., and Bourgeois, L. J., III. "How Management Teams Can Have A Good Fight." *Harvard Business Review,* 1997, 75(4), 77–84.

Fernandez, J. P. *The Diversity Advantage.* San Francisco: New Lexington Press, 1993.

Fisher, R., and Ury, W., with B. Patton (ed.). *Getting to Yes: Negotiating Agreement Without Giving In,* Second Edition. New York: Penguin Books, 1991.

Gundling, E. *The 3M Way to Innovation: Balancing People and Profit.* Tokyo: Kodansha International, 2000.

Harvey, J. B. *The Abilene Paradox and Other Meditations on Management.* San Francisco: Jossey-Bass, 1996.

Hirshberg, J. *The Creative Priority: Driving Innovative Business in the Real World.* New York: Harper Business, 1998.

Hoffer, E. Quoted in Leonard Silk, "On Managing Creativity," *Business Month,* 1989, 133(4).

Hogan, R. C., and Champagne. "Personal Style Inventory." King of Prussia: HRDQ, 1979.

Ignatieff, M. "The Rights Revolution." Toronto: M. Ignatieff and the Canadian Broadcasting Corporation, Feb. 26, 2000. Radio.

Janis, I. L. *Victims of Groupthink.* Boston: Houghton Mifflin, 1972.

Janis, I. L. *Crucial Decisions: Leadership in Policymaking and Crisis Management.* New York: Free Press, 1989.

Mayer, B. *The Dynamics of Conflict Resolution: A Practitioner's Guide.* San Francisco: Jossey-Bass, 2000.

Mongeau, P. A., and Morr, M. C. "Reconsidering Brainstorming." *Group Facilitation,* 1999, *1*(1).

Osborn, A. F. *Applied Imagination: Principles and Procedures of Creative Problem Solving.* New York: Scribner, 1963.

Pascale, R. T. *Managing on the Edge: How the Smartest Companies Use Conflict to Stay Ahead.* New York: Simon & Schuster, 1990.

Peters, T. J., and Waterman, R. H. *In Search of Excellence: Lessons from America's Best-Run Companies.* New York: Warner Books, 1982.

Senge, P. "Turning the Creative Tension On" (interview with Bill Staples). *Edges,* 2000, *12*(1), 8–10.

Southworth, N. "Canadian Team Builders Turn U.S. Heads." *Globe and Mail,* Aug. 28, 2000, p. B8.

Tannen, D. *Talking from 9 to 5.* New York: Morrow, 1994.

Tannen, D. *The Argument Culture: Stopping America's War of Words.* New York: Ballantine, 1999.

Thomas, K. W., and Kilmann, K. W. *Thomas-Kilmann Conflict Mode Instrument.* Palo Alto, Calif.: Consulting Psychologists Press, 1974.

Tjosvold, D. *The Conflict-Positive Organization: Stimulate Diversity and Create Unity.* Reading, Mass.: Addison-Wesley, 1992.

Tjosvold, D., and Tjosvold, M. M. *Psychology for Leaders: Using Motivation, Conflict and Power to Manage More Effectively.* New York: Wiley, 1995.

Ury, W. *Getting Past No.* New York: Bantam Books, 1991.

RESOURCE GUIDE TO MATERIALS ON CONFLICT, CREATIVITY, AND TEAMS

Note: The following is by no means an exhaustive list of materials on these subjects, nor does the list represent the recommendations of any of the authors. It is simply a sample of resources that can be found on the Internet or in libraries.

VIDEOS, DISKETTES, CD-ROMS, AND ON-LINE JOURNALS

Jossey-Bass Publishers (http://www.josseybass.com/)

Video Arts (http://www.videoarts.co.uk/)
"Agreed! Getting Others to See Things Your Way," 1990.

"Interpersonal Howlers," 1997.

"From 'No' to 'Yes,'" 1988.

(With Belbin Associates), "Selecting the Perfect Team: Utilising Internal and External Resources," 1993.

The American Society for Training and Development (https://www.astd.org)
"Teams that Work" (CD-ROM).

Biech, E. "The ASTD Trainer's Sourcebook Creativity & Innovation."

HRD Press (http://www.hrdpress.com/)
Asherman, I. G. "50+ Activities to Teach Negotiation."

Hiam, A. W. "Flex Style Negotiating—Assessment Set."

Kearny, L. "Facilitator's Tool Kit: Tools and Techniques for Generating Ideas and Making Decisions in Groups."

Human Technology, Inc. "Team Communications: Unleash the Power and Potential of Work Teams" (disk with manual).

"Performance Skills Teams Workshops: Resolving Team Conflicts" (course on disk).

"Performance Skills Teams Workshops: Making Team Meetings Work" (course on disk).

National Training Laboratories (http://www.ntl.org/activities-publications-ntl.asp)
Cross, E. Y., and White, M. B. "The Diversity Factor: Capturing the Competitive Advantage of a Changing Workforce."

Luft, J. "Group Processes: An Introduction to Group Dynamics."

Nuemann, J. E., Holti, R., and Standing, H. "Change Everything at Once! The Tavistock Institute's Guide to Teamwork in Manufacturing."

Reddy, W. B. "Group Level Team Assessment: A 10-Step Sequence to a Committed Team."

The OD Network (http://www.odnetwork.org/)
OD Practitioner: Journal of the National Organization Development Network. Pelham, N.Y.: The Network (on-line resources and journal).

Advanced Research Management Consultants (http://www.armc-hr.com/home.html)
"Building a Diverse Workforce for the Global Millennium" (video series), 1999.

Program on Negotiation (videos). Harvard University (http://www.pon.org/)
Harvard Negotiation Project. "Negotiating Corporate Change."

Harvard Negotiation Project. "The HackerStar Negotiation."

Patton, B. "In the Shadow of the City."

Knowledge Web Videos (http://www.knowledgeweb.co.za/)
Programme Style. "Diversity Management."

Briefings Publishing Group. "Resolving Conflicts: Strategies for a Winning Team."

Briefings Publishing Group. "How to Tap Employee Idea Power."

Kantola Programme. "The Art of Resolving Conflicts in the Workplace."

Melrose. "A Tale of 'O.'"

Seven Dimensions. "Cross-Cultural Communication Skills."

Center for Public Resources (CPR) Institute for Dispute Resolution (http://www.cpradr.org/)

CPR Institute. "Mediation in Action: Resolving a Complex Business Dispute" (video), 1994.

"What's the Alternative?" (video), 1990.

"Alternatives" (newsletter).

Journal of Conflict Resolution: A Journal of the Peace Science (http://www.sagepub.co.uk)

OTHER WEBSITES ON DISPUTE RESOLUTION IN ORGANIZATIONS

American Bar Association: Dispute Resolution Section (http://www.abanet.org/dispute/)

Arbitration and Mediation Institute of Canada http://www.amic.org

Association for Conflict Resolution http://www.spidr.org/pubs.htm

Business ADR: The Canadian Foundation for Dispute Resolution
http://www.cfdr.org/

Dispute Resolution Resources
http://dwp.bigplanet.com/johnl123/
disputeresolutionresources1/

Mediation Information and Resource Center
http://www.mediate.com (contains over 700 articles on
mediation)

BOOKS

Andert-Schmidt, D. *Managing Our Differences: Meeting the
Demands of Diversity.* Shawnee Mission, Kan.: National Press
Publications, 1995.

Brown, C. D., Snedeker, C. C., and Sykes, B. (eds.). *Conflict and
Diversity.* Cresskill, N.J.: Hampton Press, 1997.

Bolton, R., and Bolton, D. *People Styles at Work.* New York:
AMACOM, 1996.

Briggs, M. I. *Introduction to Type.* Palo Alto, Calif.: Consulting Psychologists Press, 1985.

Burke, T., and Genn-Bash, A. *Competition in Theory and Practice.*
London: Croom Helm, 1998.

Birkhoff, J., Mitchell, C., and Schirch, L. (eds.). *Annotated Biblio-
graphy of Conflict Analysis and Resolution.* Fairfax, Va.: Institute for Conflict Analysis and Resolution, George Mason
University, 1995.

Cloke, K., and Goldsmith, J. *Resolving Conflicts at Work: A Complete Guide for Everyone on the Job.* San Francisco: Jossey-Bass, 2000.

Doyle, M., and Straus, D. *How to Make Meetings Work!* New York: Berkley, 1993.

Fisher, R., and Brown, S. *Getting Together: Building Relationships As We Negotiate.* Boston: Houghton Mifflin, 1988.

Handy, C. *The Age of Paradox.* Boston: Harvard Business School Press, 1995.

Kheel, T. W. *The Keys to Conflict Resolution.* New York: Four Walls Eight Windows, 1999.

Moore, C. *The Mediation Process: Practical Strategies for Resolving Conflict.* (2nd ed.) San Francisco: Jossey-Bass, 1996.

Pascale, R. T., Milleman, M., and Gioja, L. *Surfing the Edge of Chaos: The Laws of Nature and the New Laws of Business.* New York: Crown Business, 2000.

ABOUT THE AUTHORS

Sy Landau is a professional mediator and a trainer in alternative dispute resolution. He is a professional engineer, a certified professional consultant to management and a certified human resources professional. Sy received his Bachelor of Applied Science degree from the University of Toronto and his M.B.A. from the University of Michigan.

Sy is president of Organizational Strategies Group, Inc., a management consulting firm that specializes in the resolution of difficult workplace conflicts that create tension and reduce productivity. He has also trained thousands of members of public and private sector organizations in conflict management and negotiation. Before forming Organizational Strategies Group in 1986, Sy was human resources vice president for a large financial institution for thirteen years.

In 1999 Sy participated in a "citizen diplomacy" mission to Israel, the West Bank, and Gaza to facilitate communication between Israelis and Palestinians across the entire range of the political spectrum.

He is a member of the Association for Conflict Resolution and of the employment section of the Arbitration and Mediation Institute of Ontario. He is on the roster of the Ontario Mandatory Mediation Program, Toronto, and mediates civil litigation disputes of all kinds.

Barbara Landau is a psychologist, lawyer, trainer, and mediator who is experienced in resolving workplace, commercial, and family law disputes. She is a chartered mediator, a certified comprehensive family mediator, and a roster mediator of the Ontario Mandatory Mediation Program, Toronto. Barbara has held executive positions in several Canadian and U.S. mediation associations (Arbitration and Mediation Institute of Ontario, Academy of Family Mediators, Canadian Bar Association [ADR Section], and the Ontario Association for Family Mediation).

Under the name Cooperative Solutions she has developed and delivered training programs for people wanting to become professional mediators, as well as negotiation and conflict resolution programs for managers. In addition she offers training in collaborative law and family mediation; she offers workshops that address issues of abuse, race, gender, and cultural differences that underlie many workplace conflicts. These programs have taken place across the United States and Canada, as well as England, Ireland, Scotland, Israel, Germany, and South Africa.

Barbara received her Ph.D. in psychology from the University of Michigan, her LL.B. from the University of Toronto, and her LL.M. from Osgoode Hall Law School. Before taking her law degrees, she had considerable management experience in several health care organizations.

Barbara has coauthored one book and edited another; she has published numerous articles on mediation and conflict resolution. She has been granted the lifetime title of Fellow of the Canadian Psychological Association, awarded for her outstanding contribution to clinical psychology.

In 1999 Barbara participated in a "citizen diplomacy" mission to Israel, the West Bank, and Gaza to listen compassionately to Israelis and Palestinians across the entire political spectrum as a step toward reconciliation of their deep-rooted conflicts.

Daryl Landau is a dispute resolution consultant with Organizational Strategies Group. He received an M.A. in diplomatic history from McMaster University and an M.S. in conflict analysis and resolution from George Mason University in Virginia. In addition to helping organizations deal with conflict, Daryl has helped coach thousands of new mediators in public training programs. He also teaches a course in organizational conflict for George Brown College's continuing education program.

Daryl is a volunteer community mediator with the Toronto Community Mediation Network. He is a member of the Association for Conflict Resolution, the Arbitration and Mediation Institute of Ontario, and the Canadian Bar Association of Ontario's ADR Section.

Sy, Barbara, and Daryl live and work in Toronto, Ontario. They can be reached through the following Web sites:

www.org-strat-group.com
www.coop-solutions.com

INDEX

dilemma of, 105–107; increasing mergers/strategic partnerships of, 26; interdependence in, 13–18; lack of creative people in, 90; perception vs. reality in, 18–20
Osborn, A. F., 94, 128

P

Participants. *See* Creative contention participants
Pascale, R. T., 67, 106, 143, 145
Perception: conflict due to diverse, 52–53; conflict due to reality vs., 18–20; viewing issues with future, 136
Personal interests, 123
Personal Style Inventory, 51
Personality styles: dispute resolution differences and, 50–52; four dimensions of, 49; overview of, 48–50. *See also* Relationships
Perspectives on problem, 122
Peters, T. J., 98
Positions, 82
Power struggles, 16
Principled Negotiation Model, 55
Problem-solving: alternatives to negotiated (BATNs), 57, 84, 118, 158; benefits of consultation for, 81–82; benefits of creative contention to, 143–144; as both-and proposition, 79; competition of ideas for superior, 97; creative contention process and, 116–133; exchanging commitment to, 54–55; groupthink decision making used in, 101–102;

impact of creative groups on, 93–97; impact of creative individuals on, 90–92; interpersonal conflict, 47–53; introducing process/problem defining creative, 116–117. *See also* Decision-making
Problems: conflict reframed as, 79–80; exchanging perspectives on, 122; Mutual Problem Statement on, 61–62, 127–128; separating the people from the, 162; as too complex for one individual, 90–91
Procedural interests, 60–61
Process. *See* Creative contention process
Procter & Gamble, 97–98
Professional background diversity, 23
Professional differences, 8–9
The Promise of Mediation (Bush and Folger), 65
Psychological interests, 60

Q

"Quality circles," 93

R

Relationships: diverse perceptions and changes in, 52–53; history of, 53. *See also* Personality styles
Resolving conflict. *See* Dispute resolution approaches
Resources: competition for, 27; conflict due to scarcity of, 15–16
Responsibilities: conflicting, 10–11; unclear, 11–12

Work-family balance, 28
Workforce: conducting interviews
of, 45–46; coping with
change/job insecurity, 28–30,
88–90; increased interdependence between, 24–25;
increased percentage of
women in, 22–23; increasing
diversity among, 22–24; time
pressures on, 28